Dyslexia:
Assessing the need for Access Arrangements during Examinations

A Practical Guide

by **Gill Backhouse, C Psychol, AFBPsS**
with **Elizabeth Dolman, BA, MA**
and **Caroline Read, B Ed, DipRSA**

Third Edition
edited by **Lynn Greenwold, BA, DipRSA**

Additional copies of this book may be ordered from Patoss PO Box 10, Evesham Worcs WR11 1ZW. Telephone: 01386 712560, Fax: 01386 712716. Order forms are also available from our website: www.patoss-dyslexia.org

Published by
Patoss

The Professional Association of Teachers of Students
with Specific Learning Difficulties Ltd
P O Box 10
Evesham Worcs.
WR11 6ZW
Tel/Fax: 01386 712650

e-mail: *patoss@evesham.ac.uk*
website: *www.patoss-dyslexia.org*

Dyslexia:
Assessing the need for Access Arrangements during Examinations

A Practical Guide

by **Gill Backhouse, C Psychol, AFBPsS**
with **Elizabeth Dolman, BA, MA**
and **Caroline Read, B Ed, DipRSA**

Third Edition
edited by **Lynn Greenwold, BA, DipRSA**

Published by **Patoss, The Professional Association of Teachers of Students with Specific Learning Difficulties**

In association with **The Joint Council for Qualifications**

Gill Backhouse is a practising Psychologist and Honorary Lecturer in the Department of Human Communication Science, University College London. She is former Chief Verifier for the OCR Specific Learning Difficulties Scheme and has liased closely with the Joint Council Special Requirements Committee since 1997 when Specialist Teachers became eligible to report to the ABs on candidates' special needs during examinations.

Elizabeth Dolman is Manager of the OCR Special Requirements Unit and is a long-standing member of the Joint Council Special Requirements Group.

Caroline Read is a Specialist Teacher carrying out assessments for access arrangements in a local secondary school. She runs training for special needs professionals across the UK.

Lynn Greenwold is Chief Executive, Patoss, Chair of the SpLD Assessment Standards Committee [SASC]; for a number of years an SpLD tutor and learning support tutor with additional responsibilities for examination arrangements for students with learning difficulties and disabilities at Evesham College.

THE PROFESSIONAL ASSOCIATION
OF TEACHERS OF STUDENTS WITH
SPECIFIC LEARNING DIFFICULTIES

Patoss, The Professional Association of Teachers of Students with Specific Learning Difficulties, was formed in 1987 and is now an international association of teachers and other professionals working in the field of specific learning difficulties with students across the age range from primary to adult.

Our association serves to
- establish and maintain the professional status of those qualified to teach and assess students with specific learning difficulties;
- give a professional corporate response to the DCSF and DIUS on matters affecting SpLD students;
- promote the continued provision and development of appropriate specialist qualifications in the teaching of students with SpLD;
- promote links with teachers working with SpLD students in all sectors of education and with other professionals involved in the field of SpLD and promote fuller understanding and recognition of SpLD.
- enable members to update and extend their knowledge and skills and to exchange ideas through annual association conference, bulletins and local groups;

Membership is open to teachers with approved qualifications in SpLD, students working toward an SpLD qualification, and other professionally qualified individuals, schools, colleges or organisations with a professional interest in SpLD. Among services we provide are
- a member's e-mail helpline to assist with queries relating to SpLD assessment and practice
- professional indemnity insurance scheme for appropriately qualified members, facilities for CRB checks
- SpLD Assessment Practising Certificates for appropriately qualified Specialist Teachers
- Tutor / Assessor Index
- a range of further publications including a resources guide, bulletin and newsletters
- a website with useful information freely available for all.

In furthering good practice we are very pleased to publish this third edition of *A Practical Guide* to assessment for access arrangements. Building on the success of the first & second editions, this book is published in association with the Joint Council for Qualifications (though any queries arising should be directed to Patoss). It has been written to support the Joint Council's Guidance and Regulations and provide a 'how to' guide in approaching the entire area of exam access arrangements for SpLD students in schools and colleges. It goes beyond report writing to look at where that fits into the context of what should be happening and when; whether reports have to be written and what they should include. It is an essential resource for anyone involved in the process and replaces all previous editions.

We are especially indebted to Gill Backhouse and Elizabeth Dolman for establishing the basis for this practical guide and their continued dedication to improving understanding and performance among practitioners. Caroline Read has made valuable contributions reflecting her ongoing experience in assessing students. Our thanks also to Nick Lait at the JCQ for his most useful comments and suggestions.

Lynn Greenwold, Chief Executive

Joint Council
for Qualifications

The Joint Council for Qualifications (JCQ) was formed in January 2004, and replaced the JCGQ. The JCQ consists of AQA, City & Guilds, CCEA, Edexcel, OCR, SQA, and WJEC, the seven largest providers of qualifications in the UK, offering GCSE, GCE, GNVQ, AEA, Entry level, Basic and Key Skills, Vocational and Vocationally-related qualifications.

The JCQ was formed to enable the member awarding bodies to act together to provide, wherever possible, common administrative arrangements for the schools, colleges and other providers that offer their qualifications. In this respect the small team at the JCQ acts as an administrative hub for the joint and collaborative work of the members.

All joint regulations, guidance, forms, other administrative documents, systems and procedures are produced through collaborative working and are introduced and used with the agreement of the members. The JCQ works with the experts from each of the awarding bodies to develop and agree the regulations and arrangements. The ownership and administration of the joint regulations lies with the Awarding Body members. The JCQ badge is used to denote where the Awarding Bodies have acted together.

The awarding bodies have worked together for many years to produce and update regulations and guidance for access arrangements for examinations in general qualifications (GCSE, GCE, GNVQ, Entry Level and Key Skills). Each year the regulations and guidance are reviewed and developed in the light of best practice. This year the regulations have been completely revised to take account of the advent of the Disability Discrimination Act and its application to general qualifications.

We are pleased to continue to work in association with Patoss to produce further guidance for the teachers and staff who produce the reports needed to support applications for access arrangements for students taking general qualifications. This booklet provides invaluable information for teachers and will help to ensure that these candidates are appropriately supported and receive the access arrangements to which they are entitled, thereby maintaining fairness across the examinations system.

Dr. Jim Sinclair
Director

Contents

Introduction and Acknowledgements

Since first working with members of the Special Requirements Committee in 1997 and writing the original 'Practical Guide' on this subject (published in 2000), much has changed.

The JCQ continue to update and revise their regulations and procedures to conform with the law regarding disability discrimination and to promote more efficient as well as consistent practice across all examination Centres nationwide.

The knowledge-base regarding Specific Learning Difficulties is evolving all the time and the fruits of test publishers' research and development activities are to be found in their catalogues of new and re-standardised assessment resources each year.

Most Specialist Teacher-training courses now include modules on the topic of 'access arrangements'. More teachers are developing and honing the knowledge and skills they need to assess the needs of individual candidates.

Appropriate systems for identifying candidates who may need access arrangements during public examinations are gradually becoming embedded in the annual programmes of schools and colleges. Responsibility for the proper implementation of the JCQ regulations – regarding access arrangements, in addition to all other matters – is now the unequivocal responsibility of Head Teachers and College Principals.

It has now been deemed appropriate to produce a third edition of The Practical Guide, this is basically in response to changes driven by the DDA and operating systems of the ABs rather than fundamental principles about how to do assessments or who is eligible for access arrangements. These remain unchanged for the most part. Chapter 8 provides further updated information on Specialist Teacher training and qualifications. New assessment resources which have become available since the last edition – or are soon to be published - have been discussed and included in Chapters 8 and 11. Heads of Centres now have increased responsibilities for appointing Specialist Teacher assessors. These are discussed in Chapter 4. In addition more of the process has become computerised affecting deadlines for various submissions.

As ever, I am indebted to Elizabeth Dolman for all the advice and guidance she has given me over the years. She has been my mentor and guide to the world of exam arrangements all along and I am extremely grateful for her updated contribution to this third edition.

Caroline Read's contribution is also greatly appreciated. As a practitioner, she has direct experience of implementing workable systems in the 'real world' of schools. Her suggestions and photocopiable resources are invaluable to busy Specialist Teachers and SENCOs.

Lynn Greenwold has, I am very pleased to say, kindly edited this third edition. As the main contact for Patoss with the JCQ she has been closely involved in the development of a certification system for Specialist Teacher assessors, tireless in her endeavours to develop and promote professional standards of training and practice in teaching and assessing SpLD students. This book is part of her campaign.

To avoid excess verbiage and thus enhance clarity, I have adopted the usual practice of referring to teachers as though all are female and candidates are male. I have also referred to

Special Educational Needs Co-ordinators in schools, as SENCOs; Additional Learning Support Managers in FE Colleges as ALS Managers and Educational Psychologists as EPs. Awarding Bodies are referred to as ABs. Apologies to anyone who finds these expedients irritating.

It remains to be said that responsibility for any errors, omissions or faulty logic is entirely my own.

Gill Backhouse

August 2007

1. The JCQ Regulations & Guidance – Essential Reading

Each autumn, the JCQ publishes a revised document setting out the *Regulations & Guidance Relating to Candidates who are Eligible for Adjustments in Examinations* for the forthcoming academic year (1 September – 31 August). This concerns both access arrangements and special consideration during all examinations leading to awards from their members – AQA, Edexcel, CCEA, OCR & WJEC. The handbook is sent out to all Centres at the beginning of the autumn term and can also be downloaded from the JCQ website (www.jcq.org.uk).

All personnel involved with candidates who have special assessment needs must have their own copy of the current regulations. This Patoss Guide has been written in accordance with the regulations for the period 1 September 2007 – 31 August 2008. The authors take no responsibility for any misunderstandings or failure to comply with the JCQ Regulations during this, or subsequent years. The Patoss Guide is no substitute for reading the full JCQ document each year, which is clear and detailed. Sections headed *Deadlines for making applications for Access Arrangements to Awarding Bodies,* as well as *Major changes to Regulations and Guidance* are placed right at the beginning of the document since these carry very significant implications for Centres. Detailed discussions of the roles of all involved – SENCO and Exams Officer, Subject and Specialist Teachers/Tutors, are to be found later in this booklet.

Access arrangements are available to candidates with physical disabilities, sensory impairments and **learning difficulties**. This Patoss Guide focuses on assessing and meeting the needs of the latter group. It supports – but does not replace – the JCQ handbook which is the primary reference and must be carefully read and referred to. To facilitate reference to the primary source, the JCQ handbook is referred to hereafter as [JCQ].

Access arrangements apply to candidates with permanent or medium/long-term learning difficulties and are decided well before the final examinations. There are 2 distinct types of arrangement – those which only the Awarding Body (AB) can sanction and those which the Centre (school or college) decides about, on behalf of the AB. For convenience, we refer to these types throughout this booklet as:

- **Type A** The Centre must apply to the **A**warding Body for permission to make these arrangements.

- **Type C** The Awarding Body has delegated the decision regarding this type of arrangement to the **C**entre.

The table headed *Synopsis of Access Arrangements and Eligibility and/or Evidence Requirement* [JCQ] shows who can permit each type of arrangement available.

Whether the decision about a candidate's eligibility for access arrangements is made by the Centre or the AB concerned, part of the evidence required **in both cases**, is an assessment report prepared by an appropriately qualified Specialist Teacher or an EP. However, it should be noted that their role is to assist the Centre or AB by providing the required evidence of learning difficulties, not to make a decision themselves. This is a particularly important point for independent practitioners, who may be approached directly by candidates or their parents.

2. Understanding & implementing the JCQ regulations

by Elizabeth Dolman

Introduction

The first edition of this booklet was greatly welcomed by both teaching staff and Awarding Body staff, who have found it an invaluable resource in giving advice to Specialist Teachers assessing candidates for access arrangements. Awarding Body staff are laymen and women in this field but are often the first port of call for teachers and psychologists faced with difficulties.

The move towards greater inclusion will inevitably involve more assessment and more access arrangements. We cannot accommodate more people's needs without taking on board the extra commitment this will require in terms of resources. The Disability Discrimination Act already applies to Centres and, slowly, awareness is growing of what the Act requires in terms of identifying the needs of the individual. It will apply to general qualifications, such as GCSE and GCE examinations in September 2007 but the will to comply with the spirit of the law has driven changes in the regulations since 2004, to make arrangements more equitable across all types of disability.

For some years, advice relating to the report forms used in applications for access arrangements has been taken on board and the level of bureaucracy has been reduced, as the application form and the report form for candidates with learning difficulties are now combined and the same form is used by both teachers and psychologists. The aim is to standardise and reduce the information required, so that applications can be processed as fairly as possible. People's needs do not always fit into neat boxes and it is inevitable that, in certain areas, a different response might be received from two Awarding Bodies, depending on which subjects are involved. This should not be a matter for alarm or threatened litigation. Awarding Body staff are always willing to review the situation and discuss the factors influencing the decision with one another.

Much work is currently being done to modernise the whole process of applying for access arrangements and Awarding Body staff are heavily committed to working with the NAA[1] to bring about change and reduce paperwork through the enhanced use of technology. Two phases of a computerised system have been built. The first allows Centres to record access arrangements permitted within the Centre, such as 25% extra time, rest breaks, transcripts, bilingual dictionaries. The other allows Centres to order modified question papers for candidates with visual or hearing impairment. Further developments are under discussion. You should ask your Examinations Officer to keep you informed of any news from the NAA relating to access arrangements.

For the purpose of this booklet, reference is made to **Type C** and **Type A** applications, the **C** relating to Centre arrangements and the **A** to Awarding Body arrangements. These terms are not used in the Joint Council regulations but are very useful for teachers concerned with this specific area of work. Teachers must read the Chapter of the regulations relating to those arrangements which may be made by the Centre and the paperwork required and those which involve an application to the Awarding Body. So often, people rely on what someone else has told them and then find themselves in difficulties when 'an Inspector calls'! Please do not leave

---

[1] NAA – National Assessment Agency

yourself without adequate evidence that the candidate is eligible for the arrangement you have allowed.

PATOSS and the Joint Council have been consulting with each other for a number of years. This is the sort of collaborative team-work which produces the best outcome for the candidates. It is to be hoped that this booklet will serve to strengthen the working relationship between Centres and Awarding Bodies so that access arrangements can be made both to meet the needs of the candidate but also to maintain the validity of the candidate's qualifications. It is our aim that the qualifications of a candidate with access arrangements should be seen to have the same credibility as those of any other candidate. In order to do that, we have to make sure that all candidates meet the same requirements in the examinations and are assessed in the same way as everyone else.

We hope that you will use this booklet alongside your regulations booklet. They complement one another and need to be used together. Regulations change slightly every year and you will need to keep constantly up to date in order to give the best service to your candidates. In 2007 in particular, you should read the regulations relating to reasonable adjustments and also familiarise yourself with the Disability Rights Commission's Code of Practice, entitled, "Trade Organisations, Qualifications Bodies and General Qualifications Bodies".

Finding your way

One of the problems when beginning any discussion about access arrangements is that we are entering into a world of jargon and misunderstanding. Most people think that they understand the issues until they try to have a conversation, whether this is between the Parents and the Examinations Officer, between the Examinations Officer and the Specialist Teacher, between the Subject Teacher and the Specialist Teacher or between the Examinations Officer and the Awarding Body.

Let us begin with a 'Who's Who' of the people involved.

The Candidate	This is the person taking the examination. The term refers to male and female, young and old and is therefore the preferred term used in this context.
The Parent/Carer/Guardian	This is the person with personal responsibility for the candidate. The role of this person will be explained below.
The Centre	This is the School or College where the examination is to take place and normally is the place where the course has been taught.
The Examinations Officer	This is the teacher or administrator in the Centre who has responsibility for the examinations. This person makes the entries and requests the access arrangements.
The SENCO	This is the special educational needs co-ordinator who co-ordinates the education of pupils with disabilities and learning difficulties.
The Specialist Teacher	This is the teacher who carries out the diagnostic assessment and completes Section C of Form 8. The Specialist Teacher and the SENCO may be the same person, if the SENCO is appropriately qualified to carry out diagnostic testing.

The Subject Teacher	This is the person who teaches the candidate the individual subjects and who needs to talk to the Examinations Officer about which examinations are to be entered in each series. The Subject Teacher may need to seek or give advice about the reasonableness of an adjustment or arrangement in the context of the assessment objectives being tested in the qualification.
The Awarding Body	This used to be called an Examinations Board. It is the organisation responsible for running the examinations, grading the candidates' work and issuing the results.
The Joint Council	The Awarding Bodies work together in the Joint Council which has its own Director. The Joint Council publishes rules to make sure access arrangements are appropriate.
The Regulators	Each country in the UK has regulators who are responsible for ensuring that Awarding Bodies carry out their work according to agreed procedures.

What does the terminology mean?

Entries	These are the orders for the question papers and other materials. They are sent in by the Examinations Officer by fixed deadlines. It is very important to meet the deadlines if the question paper is to arrive in time. Entries are also made for coursework so that marks can be submitted.
Assessment	This word includes the written examinations and the coursework which are two different types of assessment. It also includes practical tests, performing tests and speaking tests.
Assessment objectives	These are the knowledge, understanding and skills being tested in the assessment. They might include how much Geography the candidate knows but also how well the candidate can analyse a set of geographical data. They might include how well the candidate can speak French, model clay, build a working machine.
Access arrangements	These are arrangements made before the examination, such as extra time or allowing a candidate to use a word processor. They are based on need but must also meet the requirements of the assessment. The candidate gains marks for skills he or she can carry out, so the arrangement must not allow anyone else to do something which will gain marks for the candidate.
Reasonable adjustments	Reasonable adjustments are required by law for candidates who are disabled under the terms of the DDA. There is no duty to make a reasonable adjustment in respect of a competence standard.
Regulations	The Joint Council publishes every year a booklet of regulations relating to access arrangements and special consideration. They are sent to Centres but are also available on the JCQ website www.jcq.org.uk

Special consideration	This is a small adjustment to the marks given when the candidate knows the work but is too ill to show what he or she can do on a specific occasion. It cannot compensate for not being able to carry out the tasks being tested or missing large sections of the course.
Examination Series	These are the months when examinations are timetabled and coursework marks have to be submitted.
Results	The results are based on the marking of each part of the assessment. All candidates have to be measured according to the same mark scheme, so that their results have the same value. Those with access arrangements or special consideration receive valid results as long as all the regulations have been followed.
Appeals	If the Centre is not satisfied with the grading or the access arrangements permitted, the Examinations Officer will ask the Awarding Body for further explanation. The Head of Centre may then wish to take the matter to the Appeals Committee in the Awarding Body involved. The Appeals Committees are made up of independent people who are not employed by the Awarding Body. They cannot change the regulations but they can ensure that the decision has been made according to the rules and the agreed procedures and is fair and consistent. Only the Head of Centre can make an appeal to these Committees.
Malpractice	If the Awarding Body is not satisfied that the assessment has been carried out according to the regulations and feels that access arrangements have given the candidate an unfair advantage, the Head of Centre may be asked to carry out an investigation. The outcome can vary from a warning to removal of the Centre's registration.

What happens in the course of the year?

September	Course begins. Examinations Officer requests enlarged or modified papers for those with visual or hearing impairment taking examinations early. AB staff are busy taking enquiries about results from previous June and getting papers ready for January.
October	Examinations Officer requests other types of access arrangements for those taking examinations early. Specialist Teachers are busy assessing candidates for June.
November	Some examinations take place. Some AB staff now take summer holidays!
December	Christmas! Special Requirements Units are still busy processing but they do take a break!
January	More examinations take place. Examinations Officer requests papers for those with visual and hearing impairment, substantial language impairment or substantial comprehension difficulty taking examinations in June and sends in special consideration forms for all those who are ill in January. Watch out for winter epidemics!
February	Examinations Officer makes entries and requests other types of arrangements for June.

March	More examinations. More entries for re-sit units.
April	Coursework is being completed. Don't lose it or wrap it in bin bags! Do keep marks separately from the work.
May	Coursework marks are sent in. First Summer examinations start. Phones are red hot with emergencies, major accidents and national disasters.
June	Examinations. SENCO, Examinations Officer and AB staff are run off their feet.
July	Centre staff collapse and go on holiday. AB staff are busy grading, checking and reviewing marking.
August	Checking is finished and results are issued. Enquiries start again.

The problem is that these processes merge with one another and before one is finished, the next one has begun.

What can each person do to make sure everything is in place on time?

The Parent/Carer/Guardian should make sure that any paperwork required is available on time and is up to date. This might be a medical report for a candidate with long–term illness or it might be a report prepared by a qualified Psychologist or a Specialist Teacher. There are rules about how old a report can be if it is to be accepted. Much valuable time is wasted if parents try to by-pass the regulations and engage in a personal battle with the Awarding Body. The way to achieve the best possible outcome for the candidate is to make sure everyone knows how to proceed in an organised and calm fashion so that every application is dealt with in order and in time for the examinations. Awarding Bodies will not deal directly with parents.

The Candidate must make sure that his or her needs are known to the Centre and that the Examinations Officer has everything needed to request appropriate access arrangements on time. Adult candidates must check that they have been seen by a specialist at the right time.

The Examinations Officer, the Subject Teacher and the SENCO must talk to one another. They need to be clear about whether the subject will have tests or examinations in any of the early series, in November, January or March. They need to be clear about which code numbers to use in order to request modified papers. They need to be clear about what the needs of a particular candidate are, what arrangements have been made during the course, what skills are being tested in each subject and which arrangements it is appropriate to ask for. If the candidates need to be assessed, the SENCO must make appointments with Specialist Teachers or Psychologists in good time, preferably at the beginning of the course. The Examinations Officer must then make sure that any arrangements are requested on time and that those which have been agreed are put in place in accordance with the rules.

The Awarding Body must process the applications correctly according to the regulations and taking into account both the needs of the candidate and the requirements of the assessment. They must carry out their business with the Examinations Officer or Head of Centre. It is not the Awarding Body's role to tell Specialist Teachers how to assess candidates. Advice relating to diagnostic assessment should come from the provider of the specialist qualification.

Remember, the candidate who gets the best deal is the one whose parents and teachers work together as a team, in an organised and courteous manner and whose business with the Awarding Body is conducted in a professional and timely way.

Three Cautionary Tales

(1)   Mr. Wright is a new Examinations Officer and knows that he is facing a tough year. He opens his copy of the new regulations in September and reads it from cover to cover. He knows all his deadlines and prepares to submit all the reports which have been prepared earlier by his very reliable Specialist Teacher. Miss Calculate, the Mathematics teacher has in her class a candidate with a visual impairment. She tells the Examinations Officer in good time that he will want a modified enlarged paper for the March series and gives him the code number. Mr. Wright orders the correct paper and the Awarding Body arranges for the paper to be modified and printed. On the day of the examination, the candidate opens the paper but it is the wrong one. The Mathematics teacher had changed her mind about the paper and faxed the Awarding Body to enter the candidate for a more difficult one but forgot to tell the Examinations Officer and the Special Requirements Unit.

(2)   Ms. Phile is a well organised SENCO. At the start of every September, she sends a list around to collect information about which of her special needs pupils are likely to be entering for examinations in the current year. She then arranges for them to be tested by a Specialist Teacher or Psychologist according to the number of appointments she can make with each. She gives all the Parents the dates and times of the appointments. They go to be tested and she carefully files all the reports. She then notices that one is missing and telephones Mr. Sloth to ask whether he took his son to be assessed. Mr. Sloth says he missed the appointment but he had not bothered to tell her this and time is running out. She quickly telephones round to see if she can make another appointment. Everyone is booked up. The only date she can get is in May. Mr. Sloth takes his son to the Specialist on 10th May but his first examination is on 15th May. The report does not get to the Awarding Body in time to be processed, so his son has to manage without any access arrangements.

(3)   Miss Place is an over-worked and stressed Examinations Officer. She is contacted by Mrs. Calling-Daily about her daughter who needs a scribe. Miss Place remembers to tell her what is required and Mrs. Calling-Daily takes her daughter to be assessed and gives the report in good time to Miss Place. She puts it on her desk. The next day, a secretary brings in the post and puts it on top of the report. It disappears, filed with other documents. Miss Place forgets that she has not sent in the report for the access arrangements. All through March and April, Mrs. Calling-Daily telephones the school but the report cannot be found and the writer of the report has now retired and cannot be contacted. Mrs. Calling-Daily did not keep a copy. She telephones the Awarding Body but they have not heard about her daughter. Then she telephones the MP and the DCSF and the local press. Miss Place goes on sick leave. The candidate takes the examination but she cannot have a scribe because no arrangements were made in time.

Why do the regulations change?

There are several reasons why regulations have changed over the years. Some are simply practical reasons and some have their roots in changes of thinking resulting from research.

Over the years, clarification has been sought by Centres about how to interpret the regulations so amendments are made every year to spell out some of the sections which have prompted enquiries. The Examination Boards had to change their structure to become Awarding Bodies and take on other types of qualifications, so the regulations have had to accommodate different types of qualification and assessments of different kinds.

Disability awareness

As time has passed, different disability groups have become more aware of the possibility of taking examinations and attempts have been made to accommodate their needs as far as possible without changing the quality of the assessment and the qualification those candidates will obtain.

The Disability Discrimination Act

The JCQ regulations are being amended yet again in order to meet the requirements of the Disability Discrimination Act which will apply to general qualifications in September 2007. At the time of writing, the final version of the DRC Code of Practice on Trade Organisations, Qualifications Bodies and General Qualifications Bodies is still not available in its final version. The primary legislation in the DDA has not changed since it was introduced to apply to vocational qualifications but there may be some differences in the interpretation of how it is to be applied to general qualifications and advice given in this booklet should be received in that context.

In order to make provision as consistent and fair as possible across the different disability groups, Awarding Bodies are working towards the modification of carrier language in question papers so that the standard paper should be suitable for candidates with substantial comprehension difficulties, irrespective of the reason for the impairment. As papers are prepared so far in advance of the examination series, this has to be a phased in approach but some papers have already been modified prior to being produced as the standard paper for everyone. Technical language and abstract concepts will not be removed as these will be part of the assessment objectives being tested but the aim is to remove unnecessary barriers to comprehension by removing complicated sentence structures when they are not essential to the question itself.

Several possible technological developments are under discussion with regard to making applications, developing computer based testing and adapting modified papers to be read on screen but progress is slow and it is easy for the imagination to leap ahead of the technological possibilities and the funding needed to put them into effect. However, these are exciting times and Awarding Body staff are very hopeful that difficulties will be overcome with time and patience, in spite of the different computer systems available in thousands of Centres and the different systems used by Awarding Bodies themselves.

Why was your request rejected?

1 Assessment Objectives

The major issue for parents and Specialist Teachers is the question, "Why was my request rejected?" The JCQ booklet contains a short chapter on the assessment objectives. The major reason for refusing a request is that the candidate has to demonstrate that particular skill in order to gain the qualification. You could not issue a driving licence to a candidate who cannot see. Similarly, you cannot give a music qualification to a candidate who cannot play the instrument required by the specification, or a sports qualification to a candidate who could not take part in any of the specified sporting activities. If the examination is testing reading, the candidate must be able to read. If it is testing speaking, the candidate must be able to speak. Candidates can, however, attempt those parts of the assessment which they can manage and gain marks accordingly.

2 Eligibility

Another reason for refusing the request is that the candidate can manage to read or write independently and should be doing so. The regulations have always tried to define those candidates who are most in need of assistance, so that the reading and writing assistance is reserved for those with very substantial impairment. It should be remembered that qualifications are the gateway to employment or further/higher education. The qualification must give a realistic picture to the employer of what he might expect the candidate to be able to do.

Some Centres seem to be unaware of the fact that since 1998, candidates with moderate learning difficulties have also been included for arrangements in the Joint Council regulations.

Candidates with less severe impairment may be eligible to have arrangements which have a lesser effect on the assessment. A candidate might not be eligible to use a scribe but might be able to use a word processor, for instance.

How do you know which arrangement is appropriate?

The regulations booklet contains a chapter about each of the access arrangements you can apply for and it also tells you that some arrangements are not available in some subjects. Other sections in this booklet will tell you how to go about deciding who needs extra help, which tests to use and how to interpret the results of these tests. You end up with a list of people whose needs are all very different.

Let us begin with the most severely affected. There is no difficulty in dealing with a candidate who cannot write at all, either because of a physical or visual difficulty or because the candidate's learning difficulty is so severe that the usual tests come out with below average scores. Spelling is so poor that the reader cannot understand what the candidate is trying to convey. Writing is so badly formed that the words cannot be read. The effort is such that the candidate writes a few lines of immature prose in the time it would take the same candidate to dictate a page and a half of interesting information. This candidate may need a scribe. It is unlikely that a candidate with such problems would be entering for Modern Languages but if so, the scribe would not be allowed in the writing papers unless the candidate could spell out every letter.

There is then the candidate who has similar problems but has managed to use a word processor, is quite proficient and uses it as part of his normal daily work. The appropriate arrangement in this case is not to ask for a scribe but to allow the candidate to use the word processor. This is an independent form of written communication and far preferable to having to rely on a third party if the candidate doesn't need to. There are rules relating to word processors to ensure that they do not interfere with the assessment.

The candidate might not need either of these arrangements because she is just a messy writer. The teachers can read her writing but it is not very easy for a stranger to read it. This candidate needs a transcript written after the examination.

The choice between these three writing arrangements is therefore one relating to the current needs of the candidate, as reported by the Specialist Teacher or Psychologist; what the candidate is used to doing and what is most appropriate for the examination concerned. It would be preferable to have more candidates using a word processor than using a scribe because technology prepares them for the outside world of work, helps with their organisation of material, presentation, their frequent omissions and in some cases their inhibition about writing by hand or dictating to someone else.

The same principles relate to the other access arrangements. Does the candidate read independently? Does the candidate read so slowly that the examination will be over before he has read the first page? Are the test scores below average? Do you have to provide reading assistance on a daily basis? Is the examination testing reading? Some English units now have sections testing reading and sections testing writing. You need to check with the English teacher, as reading assistance could be permitted in the writing section only.

The biggest difficulty arises at the other end of the spectrum, when the candidate seems to have problems which have not previously been identified, so no history of provision exists. These are the borderline cases where the candidate might be performing at an age appropriate level but seems to be achieving more when working without time pressures or when contributing orally to discussion rather than handing in written work. If in doubt, you can either arrange for a diagnostic assessment to include cognitive testing, perhaps by a Psychologist, or if this is not possible, you need to use the mock examinations and internal tests as a guide as to whether there is any difference if the candidate is given extra time. You have to be able to establish by some form of standardised testing that there is a processing or other type of problem as you have to be clear that you are not conferring an unfair advantage on this candidate.

When appropriate arrangements have been given to an eligible candidate, how will the script be marked?

The scripts of candidates with access arrangements are marked according to the same marking criteria as any other script. The assessment of written communication skills is carried out slightly differently from one subject to another, as the emphasis on language is different from subject to subject. Examiners will give credit for what the candidate can do.

Examples

(N.B. These examples are illustrations only and are not binding on any Awarding Body's Examining Teams)

a) A candidate uses a scribe in GCSE Science. A question includes the information that one mark is to be credited for spelling, punctuation and grammar. The Principal Examiner explains to the examining team that the mark is to be deducted if more than one error is made in either spelling, punctuation or grammar per sentence. The candidate using the scribe is using correct grammar and has dictated the punctuation but his spelling was that of the scribe and not his own. He cannot be given the mark, as this would be unfair to any candidate who had made several spelling errors.

b) Another candidate taking the same subject and also using a scribe dictates the spelling in each of the answers where written communication is being assessed and this has been noted on the Cover Sheet. He can be credited with the mark because he has made only one error. (Some candidates are not able to dictate spelling because they have so much difficulty dictating whole words and are very slow completing a sentence. They cannot receive the mark.)

c) A candidate uses a scribe in GCE History. The marking criteria are arranged in bands with a description of what has to be achieved to attain the mark for that band. A best-fit approach is taken. That means that the candidate is placed in the band which best describes the standard of the answer. The candidate is able to fulfill most of the criteria described in a particular band of marks and uses vocabulary well to express her arguments. However, she is not producing her own spelling. The highest band in the mark scheme requires the writing to show accuracy (but not perfection) in grammar, punctuation and spelling. The candidate is using grammar correctly but has not dictated any punctuation and has not produced the spelling. A decision has to be made as to whether she should be placed lower in the same band. This would be the same decision that would be made about any other candidate whose spelling was very weak but who had given a very good answer.

How can you appeal?

Appeals can be made only by the Head of Centre. For example, a Centre makes an application for an access arrangement which is rejected. The Examinations Officer and the SENCO do not understand why. The Examinations Officer writes to the Awarding Body and an explanation is given. The Centre is still not very happy about the outcome. Before going to the Appeals Committee, the Centre should check the regulations, check the subject specification and check the results given in the diagnostic report. Only then, if they are convinced that the Awarding Body has made the wrong decision, the Head may be able to make a case to the Appeals Committee.

When can you apply for special consideration?

The JCQ regulations booklet on Access Arrangements and Special Consideration contains a chapter about who is eligible for special consideration and how special consideration is applied. You will need to read that if you have any candidates who are ill, injured or bereaved at the time of the examinations. In the case of permanent disability, access arrangements are made so that the candidate can take the examination. There is no compensation for the fact that some candidates with disabilities may not be able to do some of the questions or perform some of the tasks. The examination is measuring what candidates know and can do, not what they might have achieved if the disability had not existed. It is therefore not appropriate to try to enhance marks for a skill which cannot be performed by the candidate.

If the candidate has been permitted an arrangement which the Centre failed to put in place, the Examinations Officer can apply for some special consideration. It is a very small adjustment to the marks but it can help the candidate whose score has fallen just below the next grade. It is not an alternative to having the candidates assessed for access arrangements, as special consideration is given only when all of the correct procedures have been followed and it is clear that the candidate was eligible for the arrangement at the time of the examination.

3. Principles underlying access arrangements

In this chapter the rationale for deciding which candidates may need adjustments to standard examination conditions because of their learning difficulties is discussed.

Within the school setting, the CoP[2] classifies pupils with SEN as those pupils whose needs require provision *additional to or different from* those provided as part of the school's usual differentiated curriculum. Nationally and for all ages, and in all contexts, the DDA[3] refers to disability as a condition whose effects are *long-term* (not temporary) and *substantial* (not trivial). Both these definitions should be borne in mind when considering which candidates might be eligible for adjustments in examinations.

'Substantial' difficulties

As mentioned in the previous chapter, there is not generally any problem identifying candidates with *substantial* difficulties. So long as they have been entered for an appropriate level of examination according to the knowledge and skills they have attained in that subject, it is right and proper to provide them with the help needed to show what they know and can do. The JCQ has defined the degree of difficulty with regard to reading and or writing skills which they will accept as substantial when applications for **Type A** arrangements are made. Since all examinations under the jurisdiction of the JCQ are available nationally to any candidate whatever his age, IQ or background, the same standards regarding 'difficulty in accessing ' must clearly be applied to all candidates. This has been set as one standard deviation below the norm (i.e. below 85) for his age on up-to-date nationally standardised tests of reading and writing skills.

Centres (especially in the FE sector) are sometimes concerned about applying for assistance for candidates with poor literacy skills who would not necessarily be diagnosed as having a 'Specific Learning Difficulty' such as dyslexia. Students who have not developed functional reading and writing skills in their first language, whatever the cause (e.g. ill-health, prolonged absenteeism) still qualify for assistance with reading and writing so long as there is sufficient 'evidence of need'. In these circumstances the ABs do not require the cause of a student's learning difficulties to be identified.

In addition, candidates who have problems coping under standard examination conditions due to other conditions such as Autistic Spectrum Disorders (ASD), Emotional/Behavioural Difficulties (EBD), Attention Deficit Disorder (ADD) can also have adjustments made, appropriate to their needs, so long as these are selected from the 'menu' of *Access Arrangements Available* [JCQ Regs].

Is the difficulty 'long-term'?

Unless a candidate has an acquired learning difficulty (due to injury or illness), it will be a developmental disorder. It follows, therefore, that there will be a consistent history of difficulty and delay with the acquisition and development of age appropriate basic skills. The JCQ regulations therefore state that both a history of need and a history of provision are required to support decisions allowing access arrangements. This applies to both **Type A and Type C** arrangements such as extra time.

---

[2] SEN Code of Practice (DfES 2001)
[3] Disability Discrimination Act (2004)

It is recognised, however, that there are candidates whose learning difficulties may not become very noticeable until curricular demands exceed their capacity to cope comfortably with their studies. In some cases – and this is often found in older students in further education – their learning difficulties may not have been recognised as such when they were younger.

Furthermore, there may be no history of learning support in school for a variety of reasons ranging from shortage of resources to a reluctance on the part of the student to accept such help. Extra tuition may have been provided privately.

However, the vast majority of candidates embarking on GCSE/A level courses in schools, are expected to have a well-documented history of SENs and learning support, as well as access arrangements during school exams and KS NCTs/SATs[4].

'Borderline' cases

We now come to the thorny issue of what might be considered 'minor' or even 'trivial' difficulties in terms of their effects on examination performance. Candidates in this category will only be eligible for **Type C** arrangements – if indeed they are eligible for any adjustment at all. Unlike the criteria for actual assistance during exams (**Type A** arrangements), which are relatively clear, the benchmarks for allowing extra time, in particular, are the subject of much debate and on occasions, dispute (see Dolman 2003[5]). The problem is that the candidates in question will generally have – by definition – literacy skills within the normal range and so are difficult for Centre staff to separate out from others who are not classified as having a learning difficulty.

Many SENCOs struggle with the issue of candidates who expect extra time because they have a Specific Learning Difficulty (diagnosed by an EP or a Specialist Teacher) and yet their literacy skills are every bit as good as those of many other students. Let us consider some common scenarios:

> A candidate with a long history of difficulties has, through appropriate intervention and hard work, attained age-appropriate literacy skills and is what is usually referred to as a 'well-compensated' dyslexic. Although he makes spelling mistakes, these are generally minor so his writing is quite legible. However, the content and style are immature. He avoids using 'long' words and is often frustrated by difficulties in expressing himself. He often has to re-read text to access the meaning. 'Diagnostic' tests (e.g. phonological skills, working memory) during a recent assessment revealed persisting and significant cognitive processing difficulties (i.e. 1 SD below average for his age). Study skills support and extra time during exams is recommended.

> A student who experienced some minor difficulties with spelling and writing when younger, had little or no help at primary school as he was not 'below average' and coped quite well. He is now becoming anxious and stressed about his coursework and impending exams. At assessment, his reading is found to be age-appropriate but spelling accuracy and writing speed in the (low) average range and one or more 'cognitive' test results below average (by 1 SD). He is diagnosed as mildly dyslexic. Study skills support, careful monitoring of progress and extra time during exams is recommended.

> A student with no history of difficulties or provision is not living up to the expectations of his parents – or possibly his school. They believe he may do better if he has extra time. At assessment, a discrepancy is found between his general ability/IQ which is above average and his spelling accuracy, although this is age-appropriate. He makes minor errors which do not impair readability. His reading is excellent in all respects. A discrepancy is also found

---

[4] Key Stage National Curriculum Tests, formerly called Standard Assessment Tasks
[5] Dolman E 2003, 'Access to Assessments and Qualifications – an Incredible Journey' in Patoss Bulletin,.16. 1

between his IQ and the results of one or more 'cognitive' tests – but none of these are actually below average. He is diagnosed as mildly dyslexic and extra time during exams is recommended.

Many SENCOs as well as some contributors to the 'Readers Letters' in the national press will recognise the 3rd example and attribute it to a desire to gain unfair advantage by those who can afford to pay for a private assessment. Indeed abuse of the system is perceived as widespread in some quarters where numbers of pupils are suddenly discovered to have dyslexia in Y11! So let us deal with this issue head on.

There is a public perception that having more time to think and write confers advantage, which may well be true for many students. Indeed a study, in which the views of 66 ordinary 'non-disabled' mock GCSE candidates in Y11 were canvassed (Woods 2000), found that

> *71% reported running out of time in at least one examination.*

Furthermore,

> *86% believed they could have gained at least one or two extra marks if they had been allowed extra time[6]*

Giving extra time to candidates who do not have an unusual evidence of need for it and for whom such arrangements have not formed part of normal provision during school-based tests and exams constitutes malpractice. Centre staff should be mindful of the fact that they are acting for and on behalf of the ABs with regard to implementation of the JCQ regulations – particularly with regard to **Type C** access arrangements. Both candidate and Centre may pay the cost of failing to adhere to the regulations.

Part of the problem is that there is also a public perception that anyone with a diagnosis of dyslexia is entitled to 25% extra time in public examinations and that the professional who carries out the assessment is the one who makes this decision. This is most emphatically **not** the case. The decision to either grant or apply for access arrangements will always be made by the Centre on the basis of an assessment report produced by an EP or suitably qualified Specialist Teacher *and* the Centre staff's own knowledge of the candidate's needs and normal way of working.

The crux of the matter is not *'Is the candidate dyslexic?'* but if so, *' What are the effects of his difficulties during exams and will any available access arrangements minimise these?'*

It is important to note that the ABs do not see it as in any way appropriate to dispute diagnoses made by professionally qualified practitioners – rather to argue that '**evidence of need**' is the key issue.

Is the student who writes fluently but makes minor spelling mistakes, going to make less errors if he has more time? Can he proof-read effectively and so correct spelling mistakes during his extra time allowance? Since it is axiomatic that dyslexics cannot see where they have made mistakes, this seems unlikely! Does he have to re-read text before he has understood it? These are questions that might be answered during a careful assessment (see Chapter 8).

---

[6] Woods, Kevin 2000 'Assessment Needs in GCSE Examinations: some student perspectives' in **Educational Psychology in Practice,** Vol 16, No 2 pp131-140

In contrast, if students are slowed down when writing because they cannot think how to write words they wish to use and spend time choosing others they know how to spell; and have to reread questions and so-on before they have fully understood them, then extra time will clearly be an appropriate adjustment. Again, careful assessment which includes observation of strategies is crucial.

In short, although sound evidence of a learning difficulty is required before any access arrangements are considered, this in itself is not enough. The real issue is always 'evidence of need'.

Examinations are **qualifications** and are not designed to reflect a candidate's potential, rather the knowledge and skills he has demonstrated in the modules, coursework and final examination. His marks show the degree to which his work has met the published assessment objectives. This will depend on a variety of factors – how well he has been taught, how much effective work he has put in over the course and his examination technique; as well as his underlying general ability and his aptitude for each particular subject. Minor inaccuracies in spelling are unlikely to affect his final results significantly. There is a wide variation in the accuracy and speed of reading and writing skills across the population – as with every other human characteristic.

The clear message from the JCQ is that the only learning difficulties meriting significant adjustments to the normal examination conditions are those whose effects can be described as *substantial,* not *minor or trivial.* In other words a difficulty has to be demonstrated which really affects a candidate during examinations. This may be obvious – as in the case of students with extremely poor literacy skills, ability to concentrate and so-on; or less substantial impairments, such as a persisting lack of fluency with some aspects of language (e.g. word-finding) and literacy. In such cases a little extra time or a rest break or two would serve to 'level the playing field'.

Access arrangements during examinations are available to give those candidates with learning difficulties which significantly affect their performance during examinations, fair opportunities to demonstrate what they know and can do in each subject. No allowances can be made for shortcomings in subject specific knowledge and skills – papers are marked positively against *assessment objectives.* Certificates should convey reliable information to employers, further and higher education institutions etc. about the candidate's attainments in each subject.

There are two main issues to be considered for each candidate being considered for special access arrangements:

1) Has he been entered for examinations which are at the right level, given his *level of general ability & attainments in each particular subject*?

2) What are the implications of the candidate's *current difficulties* during examinations with *reading* the questions and *responding in writing*? How does he normally cope with reading and writing? Access arrangements should reflect his usual method of working (i.e. slowly / with a reader and scribe / using a computer etc.)

How much extra time – what does 'up to 25%' mean?

Centres may find it practical to think in terms of either 10% or 25% extra time according to need. Case Histories 2 & 5 in Chapter 10 of this booklet have been chosen to give an idea of the range of test results which can be considered as representing either end of a notional scale of difficulties with literacy to be found nationally and which would be sufficient grounds for allowing extra time.

The issue of extra time and fairness is one which is often debated. The ABs take the view that achievement of the assessment objectives is the key issue and if a genuinely disabled candidate requires a little extra time in which to demonstrate his attainment, he should not be denied the opportunity.

However, it has long been a common experience of many SENCOs that having taken the trouble to arrange extra time for certain candidates, many did not avail themselves of this opportunity. Either they had written all they could on the subject, or did not want to stay behind for social reasons – and in any case they had not been given guidance on how to use the extra half hour or whatever. None of this is sensible or appropriate. Each candidate's needs must be considered *individually* in relation to the demands of the papers he is taking and his own views. He should have guidance and practice in using the access arrangements deemed appropriate. 'Blanket' requests for access arrangements in all subjects are not likely to be appropriate. Whether the candidate can/does use proposed access arrangements to some benefit can usefully be monitored during mock exams.

The categories of disability – communication and interaction, cognition and learning, sensory and physical needs, behavioural, emotional and social needs – are the 4 broad types discussed in the SEN Code of Practice. The potential effects of such disabilities during examinations, as well as every day, vary in nature and degree. It is the responsibility of the Centre to monitor students' difficulties and needs for learning support and access arrangements throughout their time at school and college. Arrangements made during examinations at the end of their school career should reflect and be in line with what has gone before. It is the responsibility of the Head of Centre to ensure that school/college policy enables best practice in this regard. All staff, students and their parents should be fully aware of the principles which underpin the regulations and that the purpose is to level the playing field, not confer unfair advantage.

A major awareness campaign may be required to fully inform candidates (and their parents) of the JCQ regulations – and the rationale underpinning them. Teacher-led discussion and debate amongst students about special needs, disability, fairness and so-on has been found to lead to a more open and manageable attitude in some Centres.

To support this aspect of the Centre's responsibility, separate sections –

    Guidelines for Subject Teachers and Learning Support Tutors,

    Guidelines for Candidates and their parents

        are included in this booklet (see Chapter 7).

These may be photocopied and used to promote good practice within the Centre.

In addition, booklets about examinations from the Disability Rights Commission are helpful and accessible.[7]

[7] Disability Rights Commission www.drc-gb.org

4. Notes for Heads of Centres & Governors

Heads of Centres – the Head Teacher of a school and the Principal of a college – share the responsibility with their Governors for correct implementation of JCQ regulations concerning students who may need access arrangements during public examinations. Allocation of funds and informed management is required to operate a comprehensive policy throughout the Centre. All staff who teach and provide learning support to examination candidates need to be aware of their responsibilities in this regard. In particular, the roles of SENCOs and Specialist Teachers providing assessments have expanded significantly in recent years and so this needs to be taken into account when time-tables are drawn up.

Since September 2002, all schools and colleges have been obliged to comply with the requirements of the DDA (1995) & SENDA (2001)[8]. The JCQ members have – with legal advice – established that ABs relationships are with Centres rather than candidates. This means that all applications, appeals etc. in connection with access arrangements must go through the Centre. ABs will not enter into formal communications directly with candidates or their parents.

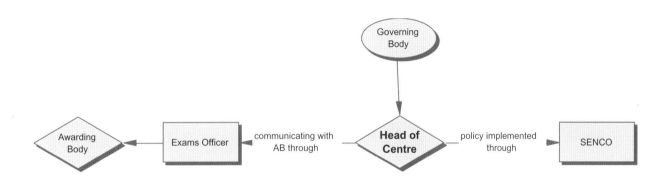

It should be noted that the JCQ regulations apply to candidates with special needs (as described in the SEN CoP) which may affect them during exams, but who do not have a 'disability' – as defined by the DDA as well as those who do have a disability. However, not all SENs will impact on examination performance, nor is it always possible to mitigate the effects of a learning difficulty or disability without affecting the assessment objectives. There is a limited 'menu' of access arrangements available, and the criteria for permitting them are the same for all Centres across the country. These can and do change from year to year for a variety of reasons and so all Centres must keep up to date with developments when reviewing policy.

Centre policy must take account of the following points:

- The responsibility for allowing a candidate **Type C** arrangements[9] lies with the Head of Centre – who will usually delegate this to the SENCO/ALS Manager and/or a Specialist Teacher/Tutor on the staff. Early identification of such candidates should result from their inclusion on the SEN/ALS register and provision of access arrangements during KS NCTs and any public examinations taken previously.

---

[8] Special Educational Needs and Disability Act 2001 (SENDA)
[9] Access arrangements permitted by the Centre

However, there will always be candidates, who, for various reasons, are not known about and so screening just before, or right at the beginning of exam courses is necessary.

This is a particular problem in FE colleges & Adult Education, where large numbers of students enrol late, often for part-time, evening, or one-year courses and do not have documentation regarding their learning difficulties or any provision made in the past.

SENCOs/ALS Managers now have a major commitment with regard to this issue. They need the time and resources to carry out the necessary screening programmes and administration in respect to candidates eligible for access arrangements including **Type A**.[10]

Historically, there has been a rush for candidates with SENs to be assessed during the run-up to the final exams. There may be a misperception locally that this is still appropriate. Is there a mechanism in place to inform all those involved that the JCQ requires Centres to identify and then support candidates with special assessment needs throughout their exam courses? The Centre should initiate consideration of access arrangements for candidates so that parents do not have to.

- Are subject teachers/lecturers aware of the JCQ regulations and their responsibilities towards candidates with special assessment needs? One of these is to alert learning support colleagues to any concerns they may have about a particular student. They should select, in collaboration with the student and learning support staff, the qualification – or options – most appropriate for the student. Selecting the right course for candidates with learning difficulties can make the difference between achieving and not achieving certification. Entering a candidate for an examination at a level beyond the limits of his competence/capacity is inappropriate. However, Centre policy should not make it difficult for a student to attend a course for the educational benefits he will gain, even if he is unlikely to take the same examination as his peers at the end – or even any exam at all.

- *All candidates* for whom adjustments are made during exams must have a **formal diagnostic assessment** report concerning their learning difficulties. *Only* EPs and appropriately qualified Specialist Teachers (Specialist Teachers) are able to produce these. Not all SENCOs have the required post-graduate qualifications in assessment of SpLD but all SENCOs/ALS Managers are involved in the process of providing *evidence of need* for access arrangements.

- **For Type A arrangements (only allowed if the AB gives permission), a formal assessment during the 2 year period prior to the final examination or during the teaching programme leading to the award of the specification(s) is required.**
- **For Type C arrangements (permitted by the Centre), the formal assessment must have taken place during or since Y7. The SENCO may review progress and assess needs thereafter.**

- Is there a suitably qualified Specialist Teacher on the staff? If so, does she have adequate time and resources to carry out all the assessments within normal working hours? If not, what is to happen? A Specialist Teacher (or EP), perhaps from the Local Authority peripatetic Learning Support Service, a neighbouring school or college, or a local independent practitioner, will need to be contracted to do the formal assessments. In any case, funds must be set aside.

---

[10] Access arrangements which can only be permitted by the Awarding Body

- Starting with the 2007-08 JCQ Regulations, the Head of Centre is responsible for determining if a Specialist Teacher is appropriately qualified to assess candidates for access arrangements. The Heads of Centre must satisfy themselves that the Specialist Teacher has the requisite level of competence to assess candidates with learning difficulties who may require access arrangements. (See Chapter 8)

  In order to maintain the quality of the process and the justification for making arrangements, Heads of Centre are required to take responsibility for delegating this task to a teacher whose qualifications and experience are fit for purpose. (See Chapter 8)

With this new delegation the JCQ clearly states that

➢ The rigour of the testing of candidates must be maintained.

➢ The quality of the reports must be such that all the required evidence is provided to justify the request being made.

➢ Arrangements must be requested only for those with genuine and diagnosed needs which reflect their normal way of working within the Centre.

The JCQ had two principle aims in revising their guidance.

1. To make the Head of the Centre responsible for the quality of the access arrangements process, as he or she would be for the teaching in any other department.

2. To permit the following categories of specialists to be able to conduct assessments of their relevant cohorts.

    - teachers of the Deaf

    - teachers who had long experience in special schools dealing with moderate learning difficulties

    - teachers who had qualifications which were no longer being offered by a particular institution

The knowledge and skills necessary to assess students with learning difficulties remain the same. (See Chapter 8)

Centres must notify ABs of those Specialist Teachers undertaking assessments on their behalf **before** assessments completed by these assessors are forwarded to Awarding Bodies.

While other qualifications may be suitable for Specialist Teachers to assess candidates with learning difficulties, Patoss, along with the BDA, feel that there must be clear guidance for Heads of Centres on which to rely to assure that assessors have the requisite knowledge and skills to assess students with Specific Learning Difficulties.

There currently is in place a whole body of training provision, accreditation and certification of SpLD assessment standards. Overseen by the SpLD Assessment Standards Committee [SASC], this is supported by the DfES, Patoss, BDA, Dyslexia Action, HADC, BPS[11] and numerous training providers. SpLD Assessment Practising Certificates are supported by the codes of ethics of their issuing bodies and a personal commitment on the part of each APC

---

[11] DfES is now split into DCSF [Department for Children, Schools and Families], DIUS [Department for Innovation, Universities and Skills]. Abbreviations for other supporting organisations include BDA [British Dyslexia Association], HADC [Helen Arkell Dyslexia Centre], BPS [British Psychological Society].

holder to continuing professional development. The Assessment Practising Certificate recognises the holder has the relevant knowledge about and experience and competence in assessment of dyslexia and Specific Learning Difficulties.

Therefore Patoss and the BDA recommend that a Head of Centre wishing to determine if a Specialist Teacher is suitably qualified to assess SpLD students for access arrangements should regard the following as the order of priority in looking at their qualifications:

1. Holds a current SpLD Assessment Practising Certificate issued by either Patoss or Dyslexia Action, **OR**

2. Holds a qualification accredited by the BDA as meeting AMBDA requirements; **OR**

3. Holds a qualification listed on the JCQ website **OR**

4. If Specialist Teachers are assessing students who are hearing impaired or have moderate learning difficulties, Heads of Centres may wish to consider other qualifications.

We must point out that the JCQ does not require assessors to hold an SpLD Assessment Practising Certificate. However, Patoss and the BDA consider it a model of good practice for Specialist Teachers assessing students with Specific Learning Difficulties.

The JCQ Regulations emphasise that not only must there be evidence of need but also 'a history of provision during the course'; that Centres ensure that the candidate has experience of and practice in, the use of any access arrangements. Do time-tables – particularly during mock exams allow for this?

- JCQ Inspectors will, when visiting the Centre during an examination series, ask to see the 'evidence of need' relating to candidates who are given access arrangements – both **Type A** and **Type C**. Failure to provide evidence of the required standard, on demand, constitutes malpractice. Centres must not permit access arrangements which have not been agreed by the AB or for which there is insufficient evidence of need.

Best practice will enable students who need them, to have appropriate access arrangements during public examinations and promote the implementation of a fair system with the same standards applying in all Centres across the country. Centres need to develop, fund and implement an effective policy in relation to this issue, for the sake both of learning support staff under pressure from candidates (and/or their parents) and of the students themselves.

5. Notes for Exams Officers

As the person responsible for the administration of examinations in the Centre, all of the paperwork relating to access arrangements for candidates with disabilities or learning difficulties will pass through your hands – either en route to the Awarding Bodies (ABs), or for filing.

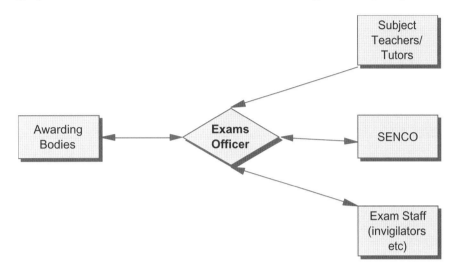

Your role in processing the information about each of these candidates depends on the nature of the access arrangements required.

There are 2 distinct types – those which only the AB can sanction and those which the Centre decides about, on behalf of the AB. For convenience, we refer to them throughout this booklet as:

- **Type A** The Centre must apply to the **A**warding Body for permission to make these arrangements.

- **Type C** The Awarding Body has delegated the decision regarding this type of arrangement to the **C**entre.

There is a *Synopsis of Access Arrangements and Eligibility and/or Evidence Requirement* right at the beginning of the JCQ Regulations showing which arrangements are either **Type A** or **C**.

The *Deadlines for Making Applications* are also right at the beginning of the booklet and these are the dates from which you must work *backwards* to ensure that all the paperwork is completed and processed in good time. There is also a very useful on-line Key Dates Calendar which has been developed collaboratively by the NAA and ABs. This tool lists all the dates in relation to access arrangements and modified papers for the coming academic year and is an invaluable tool for Exams Officers.

Type A

Close liaison with the SENCO/ALS Manager and Subject and Specialist Teachers is necessary if the system is to work properly (see 'Cautionary Tales', Chapter 2).

Time spent planning a flow-chart of who should do what and when throughout the year will be time and trouble saved in the long run.

Everyone involved should be alerted to the closing dates – see 'Deadlines' [JCQ], and on-line via the NAA Key Dates Calendar.

The EP or Specialist Teacher who will do the Section C report on Form 8 JCQ/AA/LD, needs notice and time to carry out each assessment and write it up.

The SENCO has to complete Section A beforehand and Section B afterwards.

ABs are not able to process late applications.

You will, in general, be collating and processing applications during the autumn term.

Access arrangements should be agreed and in place at the beginning – not at the end – of examination courses, whether the candidate has embarked on a one or two year course.

These arrangements apply to course-work as well as modules and final exams and so need to be agreed in good time.

In colleges and 6th forms where many students take 1-year courses, there will be some urgency during the autumn term – particularly if students have any exams during the winter series.

Applications for modified papers should always be processed for each examination series by the deadline in the JCQ Regulations booklet. Please note, these may be earlier than the date of entry. It may also be useful for Exams Officers to check that the modified paper requests and actual entries made to an AB match. Where a mismatch has occurred or amendments have subsequently been made to a candidate's entries, thus impacting on the order(s) for modified papers, the Awarding Body must be contacted as soon as possible. This is important, as the NAA tool is not linked to ABs entry systems (see 'Cautionary Tales', Chapter 2).

You will need to submit to the JCQ a list of **all** Specialist Teacher assessors who supply assessments for access arrangements for your Centre. Centres must inform JCQ **before** forwarding assessments completed by these assessors to Awarding Bodies. The new Form 8A at the back of the JCQ Regulations, or the on-line facility now available, should be used for this purpose. If a Centre is employing the services of a suitably qualified teacher who does not teach in the Centre, they will have to notify that person to the JCQ via Form 8A [or the on-line tool] as contracted to work for them.

At present Centres should submit their Forms 8A by July 15 in advance of the current academic year. The JCQ have developed an electronic on-line submission of Form 8A. This facility was made available for use by examination Centres during September 2007. Centres can use this facility to add, amend, and view their list of Specialist Teachers. When making Specialist Teacher submissions, the Head of Centre **must** have approved the respective Specialist Teacher.

Where a Centre requires the use of an assessor part way through the year, then the most appropriate way forward would be for the Centre to attach to Form 8 an explanatory letter signed by the Head of Centre which confirms that the nominated person meets their approval and that s/he meets the criteria as established by the JCQ. However, this should be an exception rather than the norm and should only arise, say for example, where a Centre has had a change of personnel part way through the year.

It is worth proof-reading all application forms for **Type A** arrangements (JCQ/AA/LD Form 8) to make sure they have been completed correctly and fully before you send them off. If you do spot any errors or omissions you will save yourself and your colleagues a good deal of time and trouble!

> Send off applications for **Type A** arrangements to each AB to arrive by the stated deadlines at the latest.

Please note that **Type A** arrangements must NOT be effected unless permission has been granted. Awarding bodies can only make decisions if they receive *all* the information they need, in a form they can access and in good time.

As letters come back from the AB granting/not granting **Type A** access arrangements, photocopy them – keep one on file & give one to the SENCO.

Type C

Documentation regarding all candidates who are being permitted **Type C** arrangements must also be collated. You need to check that all the required evidence is there and you may find it helpful to design your own checklist for use in the short term. You will need to report all **Type C** arrangements, using the NAA on-line tool.[12] This tool can be accessed through any Awarding Body website and candidates names and access arrangements must be recorded **before** the candidate's first exam series of the year.

Specialist Teacher assessors providing assessments for **Type C** arrangements must be notified to ABs as for **Type A** arrangements.

> Clip all the required evidence together for each candidate permitted **Type C** access arrangements and place on file.

A note specifying the exact nature of any access arrangements decided/sanctioned by the Head of Centre should be made available to each candidate in good time; e.g. how much extra time will be allowed in which exams; if rest breaks may be taken, when he can use a bilingual dictionary and so-on. Some Centres ask candidates to sign these to show they are aware of and are in agreement with the arrangements.

> **JCQ Inspectors who visit Centres during examination series, may ask to see the evidence relating to any candidate who has access arrangements – whether Type A or Type C.**
>
> **Failure to retain the required documentation is regarded as malpractice**

---

[12] National Assessment Agency, Centre Delegated Access Arrangements Tool

Setting up the arrangements

Accommodation

Separate rooms in quiet locations are clearly ideal for candidates who are permitted to read aloud to themselves or are supported by readers, scribes, prompters etc. However, each room will require a separate invigilator. If this is not possible, adequate space + office dividers in the hall can work well, but care must be taken to ensure that other candidates are not disturbed.

It is generally more convenient for candidates permitted extra time to sit in a group rather than in number order, so they are not distracted by the majority leaving the hall. Better still, a separate room (with invigilator) should be booked, if possible.

Invigilators and 'Supporting adults'

The information all these colleagues require divides into 'general' and 'on the day'.

General information

Prepare notes for every category of supporting adult – Readers, Scribes, Practical Assistants, ICT Technicians, Transcribers, Prompters, Sign Language Interpreters, Oral Language Modifiers – showing precisely what they must and must not do during the exams. You *must* download the relevant notes from the JCQ Regulations handbook which have been agreed and checked by the JCQ and its advisors. If you prepare your own notes you must be certain to incorporate exactly what the JCQ has advised in the JCQ Regulations handbook. Please note these must be checked against the Regulations and updated appropriately. Make sufficient copies for each helper. You may wish to laminate them for durability, but if the rules change next year this is a job that will have to be done again!

Go through these notes with your team of supporting adults to ensure they all know what they can and must *not* do.

It is helpful to prepare a matching information sheet for the candidates, so that they know exactly what the helper can and cannot do for them during the exam.

A complete time-table showing all the candidates with access arrangements, which room they will be in (book the rooms first!), the name of the helper, start & finish times for each day is extremely helpful for both students – displayed somewhere prominent; and for colleagues – in the staff room.

Information needed on the day of the examination

A system is required for collecting the papers from the examination hall and distributing them to all the separate rooms at the beginning of each exam.

Give relevant cover sheets (for Scribe, Practical Assistant, Word Processor, Transcript, Sign Language Interpreters, Oral Language Modifiers), to staff **prior to the exam** and ask them to complete and sign them immediately afterwards.

Then all the exam papers and scripts, plus completed cover sheets, must be collected at the end and returned to you.

If access arrangements applied for and permitted by the AB are not used, please attach the cover note to the candidate's work plus the ABs letter of agreement in the usual way, but mark it clearly: SCRIBE (or READER, WORD-PROCESSOR etc.) **NOT USED**.

All invigilators (in separate rooms as well as the main hall) need to know which candidates are permitted extra time and how much (10% or 25%), as well as agreed plans for supervised rest-breaks.

A white board or similar placed in the corridor outside rooms being used for exams will reinforce the 'Do not enter' signs on the doors.

Completing the Process

These are some important things to wrap up the process.

- Collect and review feedback sheets from invigilators (see Chapter 6) so you can evaluate the effectiveness of all arrangements.

- Check your paperwork and be sure all is on file supporting all access arrangements, **Type A** or **Type C**, that were granted over the year.

- Make sure your team of Specialist Teacher assessors is lined up for next year and complete Form 8A notifying the AB of their names and qualifications.

Then you will be ready for next year!

But remember:

AT THE BEGINNING OF EACH ACADEMIC YEAR, CHECK THE NEW ISSUE OF THE JCQ 'REGULATIONS AND GUIDANCE' AND NOTE ANY CHANGES.

DURING THE YEAR CHECK THE JCQ WEBSITE FOR ANY AMENDMENTS.

6. Notes for SENCOs / ALS Managers

Your role is pivotal in managing access arrangements for candidates who may need some adjustment to the normal conditions during public examinations. These students should be identified – *at the beginning* (not at the end) of examination courses. So an effective screening programme must be planned. Caroline Read considers this issue for schools in 'The SENCO's Year' below.

An equivalent time-table in **FE Colleges** and Adult Education will be more compressed and often can only be implemented during the first week of the courses, although it may be possible during course preview days in the preceding term. Many colleges use published screening materials to establish the approximate level at which the student is working. It is very difficult to screen effectively across the enormous range of learners attending FE – ranging from those on Access to HE courses to students working at Entry level, but Morris & White[13] suggest an informal way to do this effectively without embarrassing or patronising anyone.

Prior to induction, information about learning support and the possibility of access arrangements can be included in college booklets which give information about courses and also mentioned during talks at open days. Application forms may have a section for the student to indicate a potential need.

In both school and college environments a key issue is student (and parent) awareness of the rationale for the JCQ regulations, as well as an alert and informed community of teaching staff. A good deal of misinformation and hearsay still exists about access arrangements – who may be eligible for them, who can prepare the necessary reports and when these have to be done. The Guidelines for Candidates and for Subject Teachers/Tutors (see Chapter 7) may be copied and distributed within your institution (on eye-catching coloured paper!) to aid wider understanding.

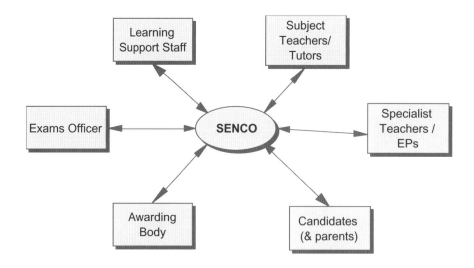

---

[13] Morris K and White A 'Further and Higher Education' in Backhouse G and Morris K 2005 **Dyslexia? Assessing and Reporting, the Patoss Guide** London, Hodder Murray

It is particularly important to note that **Type A** access arrangements apply to modules and **course work** as well as final examinations. Therefore, if a student is permitted a scribe (because this is his normal way of working) and his parents have normally fulfilled this function for homework, an alternative scribe must be found for GCSE, since 'On no account may a relative, friend or peer of the candidate be used as a scribe'. [JCQ]

The principles concerning the regulations which apply to Key Skills and Entry Level qualifications mirror those for GCSE etc. Use of readers, scribes etc. must be reported and cover notes attached to portfolios which are verified/moderated. However, the requirements concerning the evidence required – especially for Entry level – are less stringent [JCQ].

Please take particular note of the JCQ rules regarding when reports should be done and by whom:

> Candidates requiring **Type A** access arrangements must be assessed within the 2 years preceding the final examination or during the teaching programme leadng to the award of the specification. The assessment must be done & Section C of Form 8 (JCQ/AA/LD) filled in, by an EP or appropriately qualified Specialist Teacher [see Chapter 8]. The process is started and completed however, in the Centre. Section A of Form 8 must be completed by you or a colleague **before** the candidate has his formal assessment. Completion of Section B is also a Centre responsibility and is done **after** the assessment report has been received and discussed.

Candidates who may be eligible for **Type C** arrangements must be assessed during or after Y7 (the 'secondary school period'), by an EP or appropriately qualified Specialist Teacher [see Chapter 8]. This may well be the first time the student has had a formal diagnostic assessment, or it may be a review of progress. Whichever it is, diagnosis or confirmation of learning difficulties is necessary, but not sufficient. It is the effect of the student's learning difficulty or disability in the examination which must be considered. The evidence will be based on **current need** and should reflect his normal way of working. Supporting diagnostic assessment evidence is particularly important for **Type C** candidates because their literacy skills will not necessarily be below the average range. Collating this evidence is the responsibility of the Centre (see Chapter 8).

> It is the Centre's responsibility to decide whether the candidate is eligible for any **Type C** arrangement (e.g. extra time) which is justified and permitted under the JCQ regulations. Centre staff must base their decision on evidence of current need. How does the candidate normally work? How is he supported? How does he cope with internal assessments, such as mock examinations? If the formal assessment by a Specialist Teacher or EP was done during KS3, Centre staff may choose to assess **current** reading and writing competence themselves, to aid their decision.[14]

Feedback

Information about the effectiveness of all the arrangements made is valuable for both staff and students. I am grateful to Roger Lewis[15] for the idea of a useful feedback sheet Figure 6.1. (It includes issues to do with accommodation and information for staff involved and should therefore be made available to the Exams Officer.)

---

[14] For test information see Chapter 11
[15] SpLD Base Team Leader, Francis Combe School and Community College, Watford, Herts.

If used during the mock exams by all colleagues invigilating and assisting:

- Any inconveniences or problems experienced by staff can be sorted out before the final exams and avoided in subsequent years.

- Staff will be able to discuss how (whether) the access arrangements were used with each candidate and make final decisions as to what is the most effective adjustment. Candidates permitted extra time in mock exams might be provided with a different colour pen to use during the additional time allowance. The use made of this adjustment can then be monitored and evaluated.

The specialists' reports together with the evidence of need relating to each candidate must be collated and placed on file and available for inspection (see Chapter 5).

For the sake of clarity, the roles of SENCO and appropriately qualified Specialist Teacher have been differentiated here. It is often the case that the SENCO and/or one of her colleagues are qualified to carry out the required formal assessments of learning difficulties. In these (ideal) circumstances, all the work connected with access arrangements can be carried out within the Centre including discussions about individual candidates.

Should there be a need to contract out the work (see Chapter 8), due to shortage of time or staff, the ideal solution is for independent practitioners or peripatetic Local Authority staff – whether EPs or Specialist Teachers – to carry out the assessments at the Centre. As well as facilitating proper collaboration, this allows an economical approach as some tests can be administered to groups – although all the students will need to be seen individually as well.

Difficult situations arise sometimes due to the expectations of – or even demands made by – candidates or their parents on the basis of privately commissioned assessment reports. All parties in such circumstances need alerting to the *current* JCQ Regulations (available online, note these are amended annually). Specialist Teacher assessors must be named by the Head of Centre as approved by them to carry out assessments. Together with Centre initiatives to promote awareness of both the 'letter and spirit' of the regulations, it is hoped that such situations will rarely occur.

Definitions of dyslexia vary, as do the criteria for diagnosing Specific Learning Difficulties. No 'authority', least of all the JCQ, is yet able, or possibly will ever be able to answer all the questions surrounding these issues! Furthermore a 'snapshot' taken at an individual, one-off assessment, although having many advantages, may not be relevant here, unless and until the conclusions and recommendations are considered in the context of the learner's normal educational context. Those that teach and support students on a day-to-day basis are not asked to agree or disagree with a diagnosis, but to evaluate his need for access arrangements given all the information available to them and their knowledge of what is permitted under the JCQ Regulations.

Feedback sheet – access arrangements

Student	Date
Exam	End of year module
	End of year
	Mock
	Public exam
	Other (specify)
This student was allowed:	S/he used the arrangement
10% extra time	Well
25% extra time	Quite well
Reader	Not very well
Scribe	Not at all
Bilingual dictionary	S/he appeared
Prompter	Calm & on task
Practical Assistant	Anxious
Other (specify)	Other (specify)

Any comments /suggestions regarding future exam arrangements for this student? Any other comments? E.g. implications for revision

Room number	Did you have all the information & resources you needed?
The room was:	
Quiet	Guidance sheets
Mostly quiet	Cover sheet
Noisy	Spare equipment
Well lit	Signs for doors & corridors
Badly lit	Other (specify)
Too hot/cold	
Stuffy	

Please add any other comments/suggestions here and your name

Figure 6.1

7. The SENCO's Year

by Caroline Read

Deadlines for making applications to Awarding Bodies: **Type A** arrangements

The JCQ are very clear concerning the final date by which applications for **Type A** arrangements and modified papers must be made. Historically the Awarding Bodies have received a large percentage of applications after the published deadline. This makes it very difficult to process in the timescale and may lead to some students not having access arrangements agreed, or modified papers provided.

Whilst it is accepted that circumstances beyond the control of the Centre make this inevitable occasionally, late applications should be the exception rather than the rule.

As modified papers have to be produced for each individual request, it is very unlikely that late applications for modified papers can be accommodated by the Awarding Bodies.

Centres should make it a priority to agree a timeline for screening, testing and administration, which will work within the Centre as well as taking into account the JCQ regulations regarding deadlines.

The first raft of applications must be sent by 30th September, but see separate deadlines for modified papers. In the case of secondary school students taking modular examinations in November, December or January this is likely to be in year 10.

It is good practice therefore to arrange the timeline in such a way that all **Type A** applications for students in year 10 are ready by the end of September.

The following time-table for screening, testing and administration is suggested:

> **MAY/JUNE – Consider which pupils may need access arrangements from information already in the Centre.**

For example:

- the SEN register or equivalent

- students with Statements of Special Need

- those who have had access arrangements previously e.g. for National Curriculum Tests or GCSEs if they are approaching A level

- those who have replied positively to a question on an application or information form asking if they may have any examination access needs

- have a system whereby subject tutors and teaching assistants can inform SEN staff of students who may need support. This may require training for staff in what is available and for whom.

If any students require modified papers, recommendations from Specialist Teachers of the visually or hearing impaired should be sought now, as applications for modified papers for November to January modules must be with the Awarding Bodies by 30th September.

JULY – Administer tests to groups of candidates as a screening process

Centres with good quality systems in place will be aware of most of the candidates with special needs. Screening tests should bring few surprises. However, tests will occasionally identify a student whose need has been overlooked, and will also save time administering tests on an individual basis.

Group tests can take place at the end of the summer term. All tests included in Section C of the Profile of Learning Difficulties must be carried out **either during the teaching programme leading to the award of the specification(s) concerned or within two years of the date of the start of the examination series** for which arrangements are requested, so those completed in July will still be valid for all exams and coursework up to the June exam series two years later. Some Centres use the main hall to screen the whole of year 9 after GCSEs have finished, while the examinations desks are still out. If the Specialist Teacher or Educational Psychologist who will be completing Section C of the form can be present to administer the test to the group, the screening tests can be used as evidence in Section C of the profile, if appropriate. The professional completing this section must sign to confirm that he/she carried out all the tests. This will save time retesting later.

JULY/AUGUST/EARLY SEPTEMBER – Mark screening tests and set up a file of evidence and information for all students who may need access arrangements.

A pro forma sheet (see Chapter 8) with a summary of the student's scores and personal information placed at the front of each file will make analysis of his need easier and will save time when the profile of learning difficulties is completed.

SEPTEMBER

- For students needing modified papers, apply on-line through the appropriate Awarding Body's website.

- Earmark as a priority all students who are likely to need **Type A** arrangements and who are taking modules between November and January. GCE 'A' level students who had access arrangements for GCSEs, whose report is now out of date, will need to have the relevant tests updated. It is also important to note there may be a need for re-assessment when candidates move from one qualification type to another as the demands of the specification will be different, and this may give rise to the need for alternative access arrangements.

- A Specialist Teacher or an Educational Psychologist needs to complete other tests as necessary with these students, some in groups (e.g. a number of students may need a spelling test, in which case administer a test to a group to save time) but most individually.

- It is important to take time during individual testing to discuss with the student what access arrangements he feels are appropriate for him. A policy decision should be made within the Centre as to who is responsible for having this discussion and how to deal with students who are adamant that they do not want access arrangements. Consider producing a letter explaining that the student has been informed that he may be eligible for specific access arrangements but has elected not to accept them. The student should sign this letter and parents must be informed. Keep the letter on file in case of repercussions after the student has left the Centre.

- The appointed person collates all the required information to complete section A of the form.

- Discussion between the SENCO and Specialist Teacher or Educational Psychologist is essential at this stage (unless, of course, the one person carries out both the role of coordinator and assessor). Though it is the Centre's responsibility to make the recommendations to the Awarding Bodies as to which access arrangements are appropriate, the recommendation should be made on the basis of the findings of the Specialist Teacher or Educational Psychologist, as well as the Centre's knowledge of the student, his normal way of working and the requirements of the subjects he is taking. For this reason, applications based entirely on a recommendation by an independent Specialist Teacher or Educational Psychologist who has no knowledge of the student's needs in school, are unacceptable. This is one of the reasons that the JCQ now require Heads of Centre to name a member of staff who will carry out assessments.

- The Specialist Teacher or Educational Psychologist should now complete Section C, and the SENCO section B of the Profile of Learning Difficulties and return it to the Exams Officer.

OCTOBER – Submit Sections A, B & C to the Exams Officer.

- It will save a great deal of time if the section completed by the Exams Officer (front page of JCQ/AA/LD Form 8) includes **all** the subjects for which the student may need the requested access arrangements – i.e. up until their final award date in the June, 20 months later, or for one year courses, in the following June. This will eliminate the need for any more applications for most students. The Centre will, however, need to inform the appropriate Awarding Body if a student adds another subject to the list agreed. It is now acceptable to enter the subject title and level. Awarding Bodies no longer require the 4 digit codes to be entered on this form.

- The Exams Officer sends the completed profile of learning difficulties to each Awarding Body as appropriate. Replies should be collated as they come in. **Type A** access arrangements must not be put in place without a letter of permission from the appropriate Awarding Body.

The SENCO/ALS Manager should now concentrate on students who may need **Type C** arrangements. Students who have a report from a Specialist Teacher or Educational Psychologist completed since the start of Year 7, confirming the existence of a learning difficulty, will only need updated evidence that the need for e.g. extra time, still exists. This may well take the form of a reading, writing or processing speed test. It could be carried out by the SENCO or Specialist Teacher and kept on file with the report, and evidence of the student's normal working practice, in case of an inspector requesting the evidence for extra time.

A student who does not have such a report, but appears to need a **Type C** arrangement will need an assessment by a Specialist Teacher or an Educational Psychologist.

Details of candidates being granted any **Type C** arrangements need to be entered onto the Centre Delegated Access Arrangements (CDAA) tool which can be accessed through any of the Awarding Body websites. This must be done **before** the candidate's **first** exam series of the academic year.

Students & parents should be informed of the decisions whether made by the Centre or the Awarding Body.

Students will need practice in using their allocated access arrangement. Using a writer in class is a very different skill to using one under exam conditions.

LATE OCTOBER/EARLY NOVEMBER – or leading up to the examination period

The SENCO needs to collaborate with the Exams Officer in arranging resources/personnel/accommodation for each examination. Also further applications made for **Type A** arrangements and modified papers for students who have not been entered for early modules may have to be completed.

DURING AND AFTER EACH EXAM SERIES

Keep careful records of access arrangements used. Collect feedback sheets on effectivness of access arrangements.

Guidelines for Subject Teachers and Candidates

All teachers, tutors and learning support staff have a role to play in identifying candidates who may need access arrangements. Therefore it is useful to circulate specific guidance throughout your Centre. Equally candidates (and their parents) often need up-to-date information on this subject. The following pages are designed to be used as handouts for these purposes. They may be reproduced without permission from the publisher for use within your Centre.

Guidelines for Subject Teachers, Tutors and Learning Support Staff

> Access arrangements are defined as *'Pre-examination adjustments primarily based on history of need and provision'* (Joint Council for Qualifications 2007)

You are likely to be aware of candidates in your classes/teaching groups who have difficulties that may make them eligible for *access arrangements* in tests and public examinations. Please watch out for such candidates each year (especially if they are new to the school/college) and keep the SEN/ALS Department informed of their needs. It is likely that some kind of screening procedure will be carried out to identify these candidates, but there are always some who will not be identified through screening tests. The Learning Support staff are dependent on you to keep them informed of potential candidates for access arrangements.

It is essential that candidates are identified as early as possible in their school/college career for the following reasons:

The arrangements should be made at the start of the course so that candidates know what is available and have the arrangements in place for module tests, course work and terminal papers. It is the Centre's responsibility to ensure that the regulations about who may act as '**scribe**' for a candidate are not infringed during completion of course work.

The arrangements should reflect what help has to be given in the classroom and the normal way of working should reflect what is going to be available in the examinations.

Applications for permission to grant access arrangements must be made to the Awarding Bodies for most types of arrangement early in the examination course, ideally at the start of Year 10 for GCSE in secondary schools. Late applications within the few weeks before the examination are unacceptable, unless there are extenuating circumstances.

Centres are required to have made sure that candidates have practised using their access arrangements in class tests, annual exams, National Curriculum Tests and mock examinations. As a subject teacher you have some responsibility to make sure these opportunities are available.

The Awarding Bodies also require that candidates are entered for the correct level of examination. Broadly speaking, a candidate working below level 4 of the National Curriculum should not be entered for GCSE. An Entry Level qualification is likely to be more appropriate.

The main types of access arrangements available are as follows:

- **Extra time**, for candidates who work very slowly

- **Rest breaks**, for poor concentration or extreme stress

- Use of a **bilingual dictionary**, for candidates whose first language is not English, Irish or Welsh, subject to the regulations

- **Readers**, for **very** poor readers with decoding or comprehension difficulties who cannot read by themselves

- **Reading aloud**, for those who have reading difficulties and can concentrate better if they can hear themselves read

- **Scribes**, for **very** poor or slow writers who cannot **write** by themselves
- **Word processors**, for poor or slow writers who are used to typing
- **Transcripts** of scripts which may be hard for the examiner to read
- **Prompters**, for candidates who lose concentration easily
- **Oral Language Modifiers,** for candidates with comprehension difficulties.

(N.B. Your SENCO/ALS Manager will be able to advise you about more technical arrangements which may be required, e.g. for **candidates with a visual or hearing impairment or physical disability**.)

You may also be aware of candidates who rarely complete tests and exams in the time allowed, but who may be missed by brief screening tests. Please keep your SENCO/ALS Manager informed of these candidates.

Please note that there is no specific access arrangement for poor spelling, unless it is **so** poor that it is likely to impair the examiner's ability to read the candidate's answers. In this case a transcript or, in extreme cases, a scribe may be appropriate. If spellings are reasonable phonic approximations, and so can be deciphered, no access arrangements can be offered.

Regulations have changed in the last few years, and a diagnosis of dyslexia is no longer sufficient to allow a candidate extra time. The Awarding Bodies now require '*evidence of need in the normal working arrangements*', i.e. the candidate uses extra time in class and for tests and internal exams.

Summary

Although the processes of screening, applying for and implementing access arrangements are the responsibility of the SENCO/ALS Manager and Exams Officer, all teaching and support staff have a central role to play in the identification of candidates who need adjustments during public examinations and training the students to use agreed access arrangements effectively.

These guidelines by Caroline Read are from:

Backhouse G, Dolman E & Read C (2007) ***Dyslexia: Assessing the need for access arrangements during examinations***, ***Third Edition***, ed Greenwold L. Evesham; Patoss (Available from Patoss www.patoss-dyslexia.org.uk)

They may be photocopied for use in your Centre.

They refer to:

Access Arrangements and Special Consideration. Regulations and Guidance Relating to Candidates who are eligible for Adjustments in Examinations 2007 - 2008. London; Joint Council for Qualifications. (Available online from www.jcq.org.uk)

Guidelines for Candidates with Dyslexia or other Learning Difficulties who are eligible for access arrangements during public examinations

> Access arrangements are defined as *'Pre-examination adjustments primarily based on history of need and provision'* (Joint Council for Qualifications 2007)

You may be aware that access arrangements in GCE, GCSE, GNVQ, Key Skills, Basic Skills and Entry Level assessments, are available to a very small number of candidates with significant special needs, which hinder them from accessing standard examination papers.

The main types of access arrangements are as follows:

- **Extra time**, for candidates who work very slowly

- **Rest breaks**, for poor concentration or extreme stress

- **Readers**, for very poor readers with decoding or comprehension difficulties, who cannot read by themselves

- **Reading aloud**, for those who have reading difficulties and can concentrate better if they can hear themselves read

- **Scribes**, for **very** poor or slow writers who cannot write by themselves

- **Word processors**, for **very** poor or slow writers who are used to typing

- **Transcripts** of scripts which may be hard for the examiner to read

- **Prompters**, for candidates who lose concentration easily

- **Oral Language Modifiers**, for candidates with comprehension difficulties.

It is essential that candidates are identified as early as possible in their school/college career for the following reasons:

- The arrangements should be made at the start of the course so that candidates know what is available and have the arrangements in place for module tests, course work and terminal papers. It is the Centre's responsibility to ensure that the regulations about who may act as '**scribe**' for a candidate are not infringed during completion of course work.

- The arrangements should reflect what help has to be given in the classroom and the normal way of working should reflect what is going to be available in the examinations.

- Applications for permission to grant access arrangements must be made to the Awarding Bodies[16] for most types of arrangement early in the course, ideally at the start of Year 10 of secondary schooling. Late applications within the few weeks before the examination are unacceptable, unless there are extenuating circumstances.

---

[16] Awarding Bodies formerly called Examination Boards

- Centres are required to have made sure that candidates have practised using the agreed access arrangements in class tests, annual exams, National Curriculum Tests and mock examinations.

Please note that there is no specific access arrangement for poor spelling, unless it is **so** poor that it is likely to impair the examiner's ability to read the candidate's answers. In this case a transcript or, in extreme cases, a scribe may be appropriate. If spellings are incorrect, but still decipherable, no access arrangement can be offered.

Regulations have changed in the last few years, and a diagnosis of dyslexia is no longer sufficient to allow a candidate extra time. The Awarding Bodies now require 'evidence of need in the normal working arrangements', i.e. the candidate uses extra time in class and for tests and internal exams. This is in addition to a report from an Educational Psychologist or an appropriately qualified Specialist Teacher.

Please be aware that it is the responsibility of the staff at school/college to make decisions about what adjustment to recommend for each candidate. If an assessment is carried out and a report prepared by an Educational Psychologist or Specialist Teacher who is not on the school/college staff, it is essential that he/she visits, or, at the very least, telephones the Special Needs Co-ordinator or Learning Support Manager to discuss the findings of the assessment. The school/college will take the findings of such professionals into account when making their decisions, but it is the knowledge of the candidate's normal way of working in school/college that is of most importance to the Awarding Bodies. This scenario is less likely to happen now that Heads of Centre are responsible for nominating the specialist assessors who are suitably qualified to carry out assessments for their Centre.

The regulations for allowing access arrangements must be very strictly observed. It is essential that:

- The validity of an award is not undermined by the inappropriate allocation of an access arrangement.

- Candidates who have access arrangements must **not be given an unfair advantage** over other candidates, which would be the case if, for example, a candidate who did not have a recognised need for access arrangements were simply allowed to spend more time on writing the answers than anyone else.

It should be noted that if the Centre (school or college) fails to comply with the regulations (i.e. allows access arrangements without appropriate permission, or supporting evidence) this has the potential to constitute malpractice, which may impact on a candidate's result.

Although Awarding Bodies are keen to allow the widest possible access to their qualifications by making reasonable adjustments wherever possible, it is important to bear in mind that it is not always possible to arrange equal access for a candidate whose disability affects a skill which is being tested in a particular examination.

If you have any questions relating to access arrangements, you should discuss them with the Special Needs Coordinator at school or the Learning Support Manager at college.

These guidelines by Caroline Read are from: Backhouse G, Dolman E & Read C (2007) *Dyslexia: Assessing the need for access arrangements during examinations. Third Edition,* ed Greenwold, L.. Evesham; Patoss (Available from Patoss www.patoss-dyslexia.org.uk)

They may be photocopied for use in your Centre. They refer to: *Access Arrangements and Special Consideration. Regulations and Guidance Relating to Candidates who are eligible for Adjustments in Examinations 2007 - 2008.* London; Joint Council for Qualifications. (Available online from www.jcq.org.uk)

8. Notes for Specialist Teachers

Training & qualifications

As noted in Chapter 6, starting with the 2007-08 JCQ Regulations, Specialist Teachers who assess candidates for access arrangements no longer need JCQ approval of their specialist qualifications. The Head of Centre must satisfy themselves that the Specialist Teacher has the requisite level of competence to assess candidates with learning difficulties who may require access arrangements.

With this new delegation the JCQ clearly states that

1. The rigour of the testing of candidates must be maintained.

2. The quality of the reports must be such that all the required evidence is provided to justify the request being made.

3. Arrangements must be requested only for those with genuine and diagnosed needs which reflect their normal way of working within the Centre.

In order to maintain the quality of the process and the justification for making arrangements, Heads of Centre are asked to take responsibility for delegating this task to a teacher whose qualifications and experience are fit for purpose.

The knowledge and skills necessary to assess students with learning difficulties remain the same.

SpLD Assessment Practising Certificate (APC)

While other qualifications may be suitable for Specialist Teachers to assess candidates with learning difficulties, Patoss, along with the BDA, feel that there must be clear guidance for Heads of Centres on which to rely to assure that assessors have the requisite knowledge and skills to assess students with Specific Learning Difficulties. There currently is in place a whole body of training provision, accreditation and certification of SpLD assessment standards. Overseen by the SpLD Assessment Standards Committee [SASC] this is supported by the DfES, Patoss, BDA, BPS, Dyslexia Action, HADC,[17] and numerous training providers. SpLD Assessment Practising Certificates are supported by the codes of ethics of their issuing bodies and a personal commitment on the part of each APC holder to continuing professional development. The Assessment Practising Certificate recognises the holder has the relevant knowledge about and experience and competence in assessment of dyslexia and Specific Learning Difficulties.

Therefore Patoss recommends that a Head of Centre wishing to determine if a Specialist Teacher is suitably qualified to assess SpLD students for access arrangements should regard the following as the order of priority in looking at their qualifications:

1. Holds a current SpLD Assessment Practising Certificate issued by either Patoss or Dyslexia Action, **OR**

---

[17] DfES is now split into DCSF [Department for Children, Schools and Families], DIUS [Department for Innovation, Universities and Skills].

2. Holds a qualification accredited by the BDA as meeting AMBDA requirements; **OR**

3. Holds a qualification listed on the JCQ website **OR**

4. If a Specialist Teachers is assessing students who are hearing impaired or have moderate learning difficulties, Heads of Centres may wish to consider other qualifications.

We must point out that the JCQ does not require assessors to hold an SpLD Assessment Practising Certificate. However, Patoss and the BDA consider it a model of good practice for Specialist Teachers assessing students with Specific Learning Difficulties.

The new procedure makes it abundantly clear that Specialist Teachers can **only** carry out the assessment for Part C of **JCQ/AA/LD Form 8** in collaboration with the Centre, which should control the process for each candidate.

This clearly applies to candidates eligible for **Type A** arrangements, but what about **Type C**? The **same** principles apply for **Type C** arrangements.

It is particularly important for all independent practitioners to uphold the principle of collaboration between themselves and the staff who teach any students that they agree to assess for this purpose. SENCOs may find themselves in a difficult position or even in dispute with parents over expectations that **Type C** arrangements will be allowed in a Centre at the behest of an independent practitioner (whether EP or Specialist Teacher) who has not [a] discussed the matter with the SENCO beforehand and/or [b] made it quite clear to the student that the decision regarding access arrangements can only be made by the Centre.

Few outside agencies should be involved in the process, especially those who employ people who are neither teachers nor psychologists.

There should be no change for those who are teaching in Centres, where they currently write reports. If a Specialist Teacher regularly assesses for a number of Centres s/he should ensure that each Centre has a note of their specialist SpLD qualifications and that the Centre includes them on the Form 8A they submit to the JCQ, as a Specialist Teacher contracted to work for them.

Note the focus is on the Centre, and it is the Centre's responsibility to see that those assessing for them are notified to the JCQ. If the JCQ does not have the Centre's authorisation to accept a report, that report will be rejected and the application for access arrangements for the respective candidate would similarly be rejected. So Centres must be more responsible for the outside help they engage.

Specialist teacher training:

Successful completion of a lengthy, in-depth course focusing on teaching learners with SpLDs in the secondary age range is advisable, as is the requirement that competence in carrying out diagnostic assessments has been directly observed and assessed.

You must be

> able to teach and assess secondary age/adult students who have learning difficulties

> knowledgeable regarding both the theory and practice of assessment of learning difficulties – underlying ability, all aspects of literacy, as well as diagnostic tests.

> able to select appropriate assessment materials in an informed way and have the ability to interpret results correctly. The JCQ require conclusions and recommendations to be based on results of standardised tests. It is imperative, therefore, that teachers fully understand the basic principles of psychometric testing and how it is used to support their professional opinions. (See Chapter 9, *Basic Concepts in Psychometrics.*)

> trained and experienced in cognitive ability testing and knowledge of when to refer to an educational psychologist.

In addition you must have

> thorough understanding of the JCQ Regulations, a requirement since 2000;

> familiarity with the Disability Discrimination Act and how it applies to qualifications:

'*the Code of Practice to be issued in 2007 by the Disability Rights Commission on the forthcoming amendments of the Disability Discrimination Act to include general and vocational qualifications.* [JCQ]'

If you completed your SpLD course several years ago you should update your knowledge and skills through INSET geared to the assessment role. Many LAs as well as Patoss and independent organisations provide regular Continuing Professional Development courses on this topic.

Several training providers have developed courses incorporating specific training objectives with regard to providing diagnostic assessments of learning difficulties. Further information is available on the Patoss, Dyslexia Action and BDA websites.[18]

Insurance

Specialist Teachers (as well as EPs) have a duty of care to learners with learning difficulties or disabilities with regard to the advice that they give. Therefore, they should ensure that they themselves are fully covered in the role of assessor in this context.

If you are self-employed, adequate insurance is clearly essential. If employed you are advised not only to check that you are covered by your employers, but also to remind them that they are vicariously liable for any errors/omissions etc. which their employees may be held to have perpetrated. Insurance should be in respect of both legal expenses and any damages awarded, should any action be brought against you for failure to make a proper diagnosis, appropriate recommendations, etc.

---

[18] www.patoss-dyslexia.org; www.dyslexiaaction.org.uk; www.bdadyslexia.org.uk

Professional Indemnity insurance is available through Patoss to its members. This is the only Professional Indemnity insurance group policy available to SpLD Specialist Teachers/Assessors.

The assessment sessions

Competence in assessment for SpLDs – both theory and practice – is assumed. For teachers wishing to refresh or update their knowledge in this regard, please see the joint Patoss/Hodder Murray publication edited by Backhouse & Morris (2005)[19].

There are a number of variables to do with when and how a candidate is referred for a specialist assessment, which have implications for what we do and say. (These apply to both EPs and Specialist Teachers.)

The appointment might be at any time during the learner's secondary education or whilst he is in the FE sector. Perhaps it is the first time he has ever been assessed, or he may have had one or more assessments previously. The request may have been triggered primarily because of impending public exams – or only partly. All of this will become clear through the background information you collect when planning the assessment session.

You should bear in mind that the report you produce may be used by the learner as evidence of his learning difficulties and the need for access arrangements, at some time, sooner or later. **It is therefore imperative that you inform the learner (and parents) that you are not the sole arbiter in this matter.** Centre staff and ABs will use the information you provide, in conjunction with their own knowledge of the student's normal way of working, to make decisions about his need for adjustments under the prevailing regulations (which may have changed since the date of the assessment).

From here on, we will consider the situation when the referral is primarily to do with exams.

Your own working context as a teacher is now a major variable – whether you work in the Centre where the candidate is registered, for the Local Authority, are working for an independent organisation or are self-employed.

In the first two examples, you will certainly be doing the assessment because you or other teachers/tutors who know the candidate think it necessary. Parents may press for an assessment, or older candidates (especially in the FE sector) may self-refer. In these circumstances, there is the clear advantage of easy collaboration and liaison with other Centre staff.

As an independent practitioner you may be asked to work for a Centre which has no suitably qualified assessor on the staff. Other common situations are that a private assessment is recommended because staff do not have the time to do one themselves, are not sure whether, or do not agree that, access arrangements are necessary. In all circumstances – but particularly the last two cited, sound professional practice and courtesy, require that you make contact with the Centre before carrying out the assessment. **For your report to be accepted by the JCQ the Head of Centre must have named you as specialist assessor for his/her school or college on form 8A which is submitted to the JCQ each year.**

[19] Backhouse G and Morris K 2005 **Dyslexia? Assessing and Reporting, the Patoss Guide** London, Hodder Murray

From the JCQ perspective, the role of the 'specialists' who do the formal assessments of learning difficulties, has changed significantly in recent years. They are no longer required to make direct recommendations about 'appropriate entry' or 'special arrangements' to the Centre and ABs, but to contribute evidence of learning difficulties. This takes professional skills and judgement – particularly in the less obvious cases.

We should not forget the dictum '*Tests don't diagnose, people do*'. Whilst severe difficulties with accessing exams may be obvious, differentiating the genuine but less severe cases of SpLD from the wide range of 'average' learners in terms of (say) spelling skills takes specialist training and experience. Standardised tests supplemented by informal probes and observation are all part of a sound assessment and will reveal which aspects of language and literacy are effortful and stress-inducing for a learner. These latter aspects of the assessment will be helpful to the Centre in making decisions about which access arrangements – if any – are justified under the current JCQ regulations.

Make certain you are familiar with the current regulations each year and the 'menu' of access arrangements which are available.

The written report

Theoretically, you will not know which access arrangement, if any, might be justified *at the beginning of an assessment*. It is also extremely helpful to the ABs if the evidence in support of all access arrangements (**Type A** *and* **Type C**) is presented in a similar way. The standards of evidence required should clearly be the same in all cases in the interests of fairness. So it is strongly recommended that you always use record sheets like the pro-forma ones provided on at the end of this chapter to summarise and present your findings for each candidate. The JCQ inspectors, who visit Centres during examination series, are not trained in diagnostic assessment themselves, but can then see at a glance whether a proper assessment has been carried out in the case of candidates permitted **Type C** adjustments.

Section C, Form 8, JCQ/AA/LD

When completing Form 8 any evidence – either from test results or case history – which cannot be included in results boxes 1-4 should be put under 'Other Relevant Information'. This might include the results of cognitive ability tests, e.g. verbal & non-verbal skills, verbal memory, phonological processing, perceptual-motor skills, etc.

Form 8 (to be found at www.jcq.org.uk, under 'Arranging Access') is designed to be completed online, then printed off prior to signing and submitting to the ABs.

You – in the role of 'Qualified Specialist' – only need to complete Section C. After you have signed the hard copy, you must return it to the Head of Centre or Exams Officer – who is responsible for completing the preceding sections A & B.

Whatever other purposes of the assessment have informed your assessment plan (e.g. teaching recommendations), remember that you are only required to report on those aspects of the candidate's difficulties which will help the AB or Centre to decide whether an adjustment or access arrangement might [a] be justified and [b] mitigate the effects of his problem.

Wherever possible, you must use **up-to-date, age-appropriate, nationally standardised tests**. Several new assessment resources have become available since the 2nd edition of this Practical Guide was written and older tests have been updated, re-standardised and published as new editions. This trend will doubtless continue. There is already little excuse for using inappropriate tests: e.g. which hardly – or do not – cover the age of the candidate(s) you are assessing (see Chapter 9, 'Choosing Standardised Tests'). You should therefore, make sure that you check test catalogues each year in order to maintain best practice regarding your assessment materials.

All reading test results must be reported as standardised scores, so tests which do not make this possible are inappropriate in this context. Since the *descriptions* allocated to various ranges of scores (e.g. average, low average, etc.) vary from one test manual to another, the JCQ have ruled that with regard to **reading accuracy, comprehension and speed**, the only test results which can be described as 'below average' are those which are more than 1 standard deviation below the mean (i.e. SS of 84, at 15th percentile, or less).

The same hard and fast rule is acknowledged to be less appropriate with regard to **spelling and writing attainments**, since there are many qualitative aspects to these skills which are difficult to quantify. However, all assessors should do their best, given the resources available to adhere to the same standards.

There are now quite a lot of resources which enable assessment of **cognitive skills** to be undertaken to support diagnoses of learning difficulties. In the interests of supporting a fair, nation-wide system, it is strongly recommended that here too, 'below average' should mean 1 SD below the mean.

A sound understanding of the concepts underpinning psychometric testing is needed for informed and uniform interpretation of standardised tests. Those wishing to revisit statistical concepts should now turn to Chapter 9, page 68.

Tests which can be administered to a group are clearly useful and will save time if you work within a Centre. This may be less practicable in the FE sector where candidates are often part-timers and need to take time off work for an assessment.

Reading skills

A primary consideration is whether the candidate is likely to be able to read the examination paper accurately, with understanding and within a normal time frame.

- The JCQ regulations concerning provision of **readers** acknowledge that reading is a complex skill and there are various aspects with which candidates can have difficulties.

- Candidates whose single word reading *accuracy* is at least 1 SD below average (i.e. SS of 84 or less), may be eligible for assistance.

- Candidates who read *so slowly* that they lose the sense of the text – even given extra time to re-read – may be assisted by a reader.

- Candidates with poor *comprehension* of language may be helped by hearing text read rather than having to decode and try to understand simultaneously, or the could benefit from an oral language modifier if this arrangement reflects their normal way of working in the Centre.

More than one strategy can be used to access text. Good use of one can mask weaknesses in another – for example whole word recognition and 'reading for meaning' can supplement and compensate for weak decoding. The latter, however, may make the candidate prone to errors in stressful situations where accurate reading is vital – as in maths and exam questions.

Reading skills may need to be assessed in a variety of ways – at word & text level, timed and untimed – before a true picture of a candidate's skills and potential needs for access arrangements can be assessed. It is probably true to say that where reading ability is already known to be extremely limited, a graded single word test will suffice as evidence of need for a reader. Where the difficulties are less obvious, a more thorough examination may be required.

Perhaps the most valid type of test to use when evaluating the need for reading assistance is one which requires the candidate to read continuous text **silently** and respond to comprehension questions, under timed conditions. This mirrors the exam situation most closely and takes the time needed to respond into account.

Oral reading tests enable close observation and monitoring of skills and strategies. Therefore, they are especially appropriate where planning intervention is one reason for the assessment. On the whole they only measure how quickly the passages are read **before** the comprehension questions are posed. Therefore, the fluency measures – whilst entirely valid in themselves – may be less appropriate for the more able reader who, whilst fairly accurate, has to re-read before he has fully grasped the meaning.

A selection of reading tests should therefore be available which focus on accuracy, fluency and comprehension and are suitable for different types of learner. Please see Chapter 11, page 91 Reading Tests Compared, for the main resources currently available to Specialist Teachers and suitable for ages 14+.

1. Reading Accuracy

An untimed graded single word test should be used here. [Tests are listed alphabetically.]

- **HORT** *Hodder Oral Reading Tests* **(5 – 16+ years)**

Quick to administer with an accessible manual, the HORT offers three complementary tests – **graded single word reading**, plus sentence reading and reading speed (see below). There are two parallel forms.

- *Single Word Reading Test* **(6 – 16 years)**

Another quick-to-administer word reading test designed for checking progress at regular intervals. It contains six graded sets of ten words of increasing difficulty. Parallel forms are provided as well as diagnostic information.

- **WIAT-II-UK-T** *Wechsler Individual Achievement Test: Second UK Edition for Teachers* **(4 – 85.11 years)**

The graded word reading test in this battery incorporates assessment of phonological awareness and decoding skills for use with younger pupils. The test is untimed, but a mechanism for assessing 'automaticity' of word reading is included. Reading comprehension and spelling tests are included in the pack (see below).

- **WRAT 4** *Wide Range Achievement Test 4* **(5 – 94 years)**

The WRAT is an American test – but distributed and widely used in the UK. It contains not only two parallel reading tests, but two spelling (see below) and two arithmetic tests as well. Standard scores are easily obtained from the manual, but be careful to use the appropriate Blue or Tan age norms.

(Specialist Teachers working with EPs may also have access to the BAS & WORD reading tests, but cannot purchase these resources themselves.)

Other types of reading test can be used to investigate word level skills. However, supplementary evidence regarding the candidate's speed/fluency, decoding competence *cf.* sight vocabulary, should be discussed in **Other relevant information** in Section C of Form 8 – see below.

> **You are asked not to note any additional evidence in the first results box.**

- **HORT** *Hodder Oral Reading Tests* **(5 – 16+ years)**

The sentence reading test in this battery enables the assessor to probe the degree to which the candidate's mechanical word recognition skills are 'bootstrapped' by grammar and meaning at sentence level. The Reading Speed section assesses how many regular three and four-letter words the candidate can read in 60 seconds and thus focuses on 'automaticity' of lower-level reading skills.

- **NWRT** *Nonword Reading Test* **(6 – 16 years)**

First developed in Australia and then standardised in the UK in tandem with the Diagnostic Reading Analysis (DRA) & the Edinburgh 4, this test has 2 parallel forms and provides error analysis columns on the record sheets to help identify phonic patterns the student does not know and needs to learn.

(The Nonword subtest from the **PhAB** *Phonological Assessment Battery* has been omitted here as it is not timed and only suitable for candidates up to 14 years 11 months.)

- **TOWRE** *Test of Word Reading Efficiency* **(6 – 24 years)**

The TOWRE yields valuable information about how **automatically** (i.e. quickly) the candidate can read words, often a factor in comprehension difficulties. It compares both real word and non-word reading under timed conditions. A discrepancy between the two subtest scores is particularly revealing. Dyslexics are often far worse at the non-word subtest due to their weak decoding skills.

The *Two Minute Reading Test* (of real words) in the **DST** *Dyslexia Screening Test* can also be used to gauge fluency at word level.

- *Wordchains* **(7 – 18 years)**

This efficient way of assessing word-level skills in a group (well-established in Sweden where it originated) is useful for screening as well as individual use. However, it assesses **silent** word recognition by asking testees to put lines where the boundaries are in strings of words printed without spaces between them. So it is not measuring the same skills as an oral test does and can only therefore provide supplementary information regarding the need for access arrangements. The manual contains interesting data showing correlations between Wordchains scores and grades achieved at KS3 & GCSE English and English Literature. The Letterchains section can also be used to screen for visual-motor skill deficits.

1. Reading Speed and Comprehension

There are several tests which can be used here:

ORAL READING TESTS

- **ART** *Adult Reading Test* **(16 – 25+ years)**

This test has been criticised on the grounds of the rather limited standardisation sample (comparatively small and restricted to 6 FE/HE institutions in and around London).

Nearly a quarter of the standardisation sample were students with EAL. Since their data is provided as a separate set of norms, this resource may be of use in similar contexts.

- **DRA** *Diagnostic Reading Analysis* **(7 – 16 years)**

The DRA, developed specifically for use with poor readers, contains both fiction and non-fiction passages for each age-level and closely matches the National Literacy Strategy [NLS]. It has 2 parallel forms for retesting and incorporates a passage for assessing whether listening comprehension is age appropriate. The pupil's performance on this part determines the level at which he should start the reading assessment. The test is designed so that pupils need only read three passages as a rule and should take no more than 15 minutes altogether, thus making it more efficient than some others. Accuracy as well as Speed of oral reading (i.e. not taking time needed for comprehension into account) and Comprehension are measured.

- **GORT 4** *Gray Oral Reading Tests Fourth Edition* **(6 – 18.11 years)**

An oral reading fluency score (i.e. not taking time needed for comprehension into account) is derived from separate Rate & Accuracy results in this American test, which has 2 parallel forms.

Some of the content and ways in which words are used may be unfamiliar to UK children and so this test may not always be suitable in this context – especially for candidates of low ability, or whose first language is not English.

NB   The examiner can supply words that the student cannot read correctly and so the Comprehension score does not necessarily represent his ability to understand text without help.

- **WIAT-II-UK-T** *Wechsler Individual Achievement Test: Second UK Edition for Teachers* **(4 – 85.11 years)**

A thorough test of sentence and text level comprehension. Overlapping sets of age-specific items are provided, each with a start & stop point. Should the set be too difficult, a previous one must be administered. The testee can decide to read passages aloud or silently and is timed whilst so doing, but the sentences must be read aloud. Comprehension questions are posed after each item.

- **WRAT-E** *Wide Range Achievement Test – Expanded Individual Assessment Form I* **(5 – 24.11 years).**

This test is best suited for use with higher ability/attainment native English speaking students. It can be administered as an oral accuracy & comprehension test and contains other subtests.

SILENT READING TESTS

As suggested above, **silent** reading tests are arguably more useful with this group.

They can be administered as group tests and so they are suitable for screening as well as individual assessments. Those that are timed are particularly relevant in this context since results will assist the Centre to make decisions regarding the need for extra time during examinations.

In all the tests mentioned below, responses to comprehension questions are by multiple choice and so no writing is involved.

Most of the **silent** reading tests mentioned below are timed. When considering access arrangements, provide the candidate with a different colour pen (or even 2 different colours!!) and allow him to continue with the test for another 25% (or 10%, then the full 25%). In this way you can judge whether a poor score is essentially to do with speed or whether he still cannot cope with aspects of the assessment no matter how much extra time is given.

However, this information should be given in **Other relevant information** in Section C of Form 8 – see below.

> **You are asked not to note any additional evidence in the second results box.**

The following tests may prove useful in supplying additional diagnostic information:

- ***Access Reading Test*** (7 – 20+ years)

This test gives useful diagnostic information regarding a candidate's skills in four key areas – literal comprehension; vocabulary; understanding requiring inference or prediction; comprehension requiring analysis, as well as an overall score. There are two parallel forms & administration takes a maximum of 30 minutes.

- ***Edinburgh Reading Test 4*** (11 – 16 years)

A total score plus a diagnostic profile is generated from the candidate's performance on the different sections of the test. This gives valuable comparative information about his reading strategies and ability to skim for information, read carefully for facts, perceive the consistency of various point of view in text, use inference and understand word meanings, useful for remedial work as well as considering appropriate access arrangements. Section B (Vocabulary) is often a particular challenge for dyslexic candidates whose single word reading *and* oral vocabulary are not well developed – an entirely different situation from simply running out of time. Standard administration time is 45 minutes; testing may be continued for an extra 11¼ minutes to gauge attainment given extra time.

- ***Edinburgh Reading Test 4 – Interactive*** (11.7 years – adult)

An interactive version of the ERT4 which the student takes on screen. The programme then calculates scores attained during the standard 45 minute test time and again including an extra 25% of time.

- **GSRT *Gray Silent Reading Tests*** (7 – 25 years)

Although this test has a higher 'ceiling' than the others mentioned here, as well as 2 parallel forms, it has the disadvantage of not having a time limit which is particularly pertinent in this context.

- **HGRT** *Hodder Group Reading Tests: Second Edition* (5 – 16+ years)

Comprehension is assessed at word, sentence and text level using sentence completion and Cloze techniques. 30 minutes are allowed for completion of the test at secondary level, and students can be given an additional 7½ minutes (25% extra), using a different colour pen to see if their performance improves significantly given more time. However, most pupils are expected to finish the test easily within the half hour.

- *WRAT-E Wide Range Achievement Test – Expanded Group Assessment (Form G)* (7 – 18.11 years)

Suitable for use with older, higher ability candidates, but you should consider whether the occasional American spellings (e.g. characterize, tumor) and inclusion of American place names (e.g. Pennsylvania, Connecticut) are likely to affect the learner's comprehension. Score twice – with and without extra time to assess the value of extra time to the candidate(s). This resource contains non-verbal reasoning and Maths tests also. (For individual administration see above.)

Writing skills

There are several issues here. Is it likely that the examiner will be unable to decipher what this candidate writes, given his spelling and handwriting? Is this candidate unable to demonstrate his knowledge and skills within time constraints given his writing competence and speed? If the answer to either of these questions is '*Yes*', does his written output improve significantly if he uses a word processor or has more time? If not, is there a real difference in the quality/quantity of his output if he dictates to someone else?

2. Accuracy & Legibility

Spelling should be assessed at word and text level. You are only asked to comment on word-level spelling in the third results box and the following tests can be used.

- *British Spelling Test Series* (5 years – adult)

Comprehensive – and therefore lengthy to administer (30 – 40 minutes) – these overlapping sets of spelling assessments give much useful diagnostic and remedial information. There are 5 levels and each one has two alternative forms

- *Diagnostic Spelling Tests 3-5* (9 – 25+ years)

Three different tests are provided in the one pack, covering age groups 9-12; 11-15; 15-20+ years. Two parallel forms are provided as photocopiable masters for tests 4 & 5. Each word is dictated in a sentence and students are then allowed 15 seconds to respond, so exceptionally slow spelling fluency can be noted. Each test takes about 15 minutes to administer. The words in test 3 are taken from the NLS; three quarters of the words in test 4 are taken from KS3 vocabulary lists of the major school subjects. Test 5 contains words most commonly mis-spelled by adults and focuses on functional literacy. The concise and easy-to-use manual includes diagnostic information and follow-up activities.

- **HAST** *Helen Arkell Spelling Test* (5 – 17 years)

This test is designed to be diagnostic but also gives standardised scores. The test items represent the normal development of spelling and range from high to low frequency words. The assessor can describe the candidate's spelling profile and recommend a starting point for remediation.

- *Vernon Graded Word Spelling Test: Third Edition* (5 – 18+ years)

This well-known test has now been completely revised and restandardised. The words are dictated in the context of given sentences and arranged in age-specific sets which are informed by the NLS. Fifteen seconds are allowed for the candidates to write each word which gives a useful indication of spelling fluency.

- **WRAT-4** *Wide Range Achievement Test 4* (5 – 75 years)

The WRAT also gives an indication of spelling fluency by allowing 15 seconds for each word to be written. There are 2 parallel forms so once again be careful to use the correct age norms for the *Blue* or *Tan* form.

The **Two Minute Spelling Test** in the **DST** *Dyslexia Screening Tests* can also yield useful supplementary information with regard to spelling fluency.

Specialist Teachers working with EPs may also have access to the BAS & WORD spelling tests, but cannot purchase these resources themselves.

You are now in a position to answer **question 3** regarding accuracy & legibility at word level:

> **Is the candidate's spelling accuracy in the below average range (i.e. SS of 84 or below)?**

However, a low spelling score can be achieved because of *minor errors* – which do not reduce the readability of the words rather than *bizarre spellings* and/or atrocious handwriting – which make it extremely difficult to guess what each word might have been. Only the latter type are of interest in this context, which is why you are asked to state the 'percentage of errors *unrecognisable* as target word'. Calculate this percentage out of the total number of words attempted.

The next three questions relate to free-writing so you must now assess the candidate's continuous writing skills. Many candidates with dyslexia cannot sustain the same level of accuracy or legibility when their attention is focused on composition rather than spelling – especially under time constraints. Apart from spelling and handwriting, they may have such difficulties with composition – at sentence and text level – that their writing becomes 'incomprehensible'.

Can they produce an altogether more readable level of written output when using a word-processor? This is a crucial question to answer as the ABs much prefer candidates to work independently and use a computer than rely on a scribe. They are unlikely to agree that anyone should have a scribe if he has reasonable keyboard skills.

Therefore free-writing by hand and free-writing on a computer or word-processor using predictive text are all necessary aspects of the assessment. You will then be able to answer the questions regarding accuracy & legibility:

> **Does the candidate's spelling and/or handwriting render his/her free writing largely illegible?**
>
> **Is the candidate's free writing incomprehensible?**
>
> **Is the candidate proficient in the use of a word processor?**

Learning support teachers are usually rather good at deciphering dyslexic students' spelling – so try to put yourself in the shoes of the English, Science or Geography examiner! Clearly a high number of 'unrecognisables' here is very telling with regard to the quality of a candidate's spelling – whereas if your answer is 0% – then the examiners will not have a problem reading this candidate's scripts.

The free-writing tasks should be **timed**, so that the questions posed by the next section can be answered.

3. Writing Speed

Written output may be meagre for many reasons – problems with expressive language, composition, spelling or manual dexterity (or all of these). Clearly, a copying task will not get to the heart of the matter in all cases. The following assessment resources may be used but **it is essential to record on Form 8** which one has been used. This is because the test tasks vary one from another and so produce different normative data. So, **you cannot administer one task and then use the norms from a different one to assess free writing speed.**

Free writing tasks of 20-30 minutes duration were used to assess handwriting speeds of Y10/11 pupils in research projects by Penny Allcock and Liz Waine[20] .carried out in large comprehensive schools. Both found a wide range of 'average' writing rates (means of 15/16 w.p.m. with a SD of 5). In view of the findings mentioned in the DASH manual (see below), the variance may partly be accounted for by students having a choice of topics to write about. Penny Allcock was awarded a 'Best Practice Research Scholarship' by the DfEE for her project which enabled her to include additional data in the results currently shown for this assessment method..

- *Assessment of Handwriting Speed* **(Y9 – 11, with projected scores Y 12 – 13)**

This method uses a 20 minute free-writing task and the method is described on the Patoss website where research results are also given[21].

Allcock has calculated the 'cut-off' points at which candidates should be allowed 25% extra time in order to have equal opportunities (cf. 'average' candidates) to finish written answers, or might need a scribe. She has also predicted average free-writing speeds during Y12 & Y13 by projecting scores from the 2001 data.

The ABs accept this method as valid at the present time.

- **DASH** *Detailed Assessment of Speed of Handwriting* **(9 – 16 years 11 months)**

For group or individual administration this new, fully standardised test takes about 30 minutes and includes 5 component tasks, covering perceptual motor competence, copying quickly and in 'best' handwriting and writing out the alphabet. The fifth is a 10 minute free writing task and a pilot study was undertaken to ascertain the topic and methodology which produced the 'best results' - i.e. the most words. Comparison of w.p.m. produced in response to two different titles produced statistically different results. This is an extremely important fact to remember and is, no doubt, part of the reason why the average raw scores and norms obtained here differ significantly from those using Penny Allcock's methodology.

---

[20] Allcock P 2001 'Testing Handwriting Speed' Patoss website: www.patoss-dyslexia.org and Waine L 2001, 'Writing Speed: what constitutes slow? In Rose R & Grosvenor I (Eds) **Doing Research in Special Education – Ideas into Practice** London: David Fulton
[21] www.patoss-dyslexia.org

Normative data across the UK was collected in tandem with the re-standardisation of the *Movement Assessment Battery for Children* (M-ABC II).

- *Sentence Completion Test* **(9 – 18 years)**[22]

The normative data established by Hedderley (1995) in Kirklees LEA using a sentence completion test, differs yet again from the results of the 2 assessments mentioned above! It is important to note that the skills of completing a series of unconnected sentences are not the same as those required to produce a coherent piece of free writing. The demands of the two tasks are different and unless the *validity* of using results from one type of test to predict performance on a different task has been established, extreme caution should be exercised. The Hedderley test will surely reveal the difficulties of students with moderate to severe difficulties at word and sentence level, but may not highlight the problems of the less severely/well-compensated dyslexic pupil, who struggles to produce continuous writing. As ever, the same assessment resources and methods will not be suitable for all.

Whichever method is used, other samples of the candidate's free-writing under controlled conditions (such as the latest end of year exam papers) might also be scrutinised for comparison.

Samples of free-writing should be analysed **qualitatively** as well as **quantitatively and** the percentage of illegible words due to poor handwriting or bizarre spelling calculated. These results – for both hand-written and word-processed samples – are entered in the fifth box.

Clearly, very slow writing speeds and / or extremely poor readability would give rise to consideration of **Type A** access arrangements such as more than 25% extra time, use of a scribe, or word-processor.

Word-processing

There seems no logical reason why the benchmarks for handwriting and word-processing speed should differ markedly in this context. The point is not 'average typing speed' since very few candidates are permitted to use word-processing at present. The issue is whether the candidate **can write at an average speed if he uses a computer rather than a pen.**

If he can comfortably type 20 words a minute – the top end of the normal range of free-writing speed, using Allcock's method, – he is at no disadvantage compared to other candidates. If he can type at 25 or 30 wpm (1 or 2 SDs above the mean cf. handwriting) he **already** has a considerable advantage regarding time, which he can use to proof-read and edit his responses. Requests for permission to use a word-processor based solely on the premise that a candidate can type faster than he can write – although he writes at a normal speed – are almost certain to be refused. The real issues to be considered here are 'normal method of working' (in class), legibility and 'quality of language'.

Scribes

If, even when using a computer, the candidate's free-writing is still 'incomprehensible' or he is still so slow that extra time makes little difference, can he express himself orally and dictate to a scribe or use word-processing with predictive text or voice activation? If so, does his 'quality of language' or speed improve markedly? What is sought here is evidence of very real differences

---

[22] www.dyslexia-inst.org.uk

between handwritten and typed, or oral and written expression – as in the first Case Study (John) in Chapter 10.

Evidence

Since the ABs no longer ask to see the evidence supporting these requests, Specialist Teachers conducting the assessment and the Centre must be scrupulous in the standards they apply. They must be comfortable, that these would stand up under an investigation. Therefore, it is essential that supporting evidence is both obtained and retained for every such application.

Other relevant information

In this section you should include and discuss any evidence or advice which will assist the Centre and/or AB when considering appropriate access arrangements – whether of **Type A** or **Type C**.

For substantial reading difficulties, such information should help to clarify whether a reader, read aloud, oral language modifier, or extra time (up to 25% or more) is the most effective arrangement.

In the case of substantial writing difficulties, it should help in deciding if extra time (up to 25% or even more in exceptional cases), word-processing, dictation to a scribe or provision of a transcript would be the most appropriate arrangement?

Cognitive difficulties – if revealed by diagnostic testing – should also be reported in this section together with a brief note about their likely impact in examinations.

Please keep your comments focused on these salient issues and succinct!

Phonological processing

Research by Rashotte et al (see CTOPP manual) has defined poor performance on measures of **phonological awareness, verbal memory** and **rapid naming** as key indicators of dyslexia. Tests which are useful for detecting weaknesses in older learners include phoneme deletion, spoonerisms, fluency and rapid naming. Word-finding problems are common in dyslexia and rapid naming tests are valuable diagnostic tools since this process is not affected by literacy **development**.

- *PhAB Phonological Assessment Battery (6 years – 14years 11 mths)*

Although the ceiling on this test is quite low for our purposes, the Picture Naming, Fluency and Spoonerisms tests, will challenge older students with severe phonological deficits.

- *Perin's Spoonerism Task (14 – 25)* [23]

Although this test was originally for Y10 students, the results hold good for older students and so the norms given on the website may be used for this group.

Timing is crucial and the time to be recorded is from when the tester finishes dictating the two words until the testee finishes his response, viz.

Tester, "Sue Lawley" *Start timing* …… Testee, "Loo Sawley" *Stop timer*

↑_____ Time Taken _____↑

---

[23] Free download from Dyslexia Action website: http://www.dyslexiaaction.org.uk/Administration/uploads/perins.pdf

- **CTOPP** *Comprehensive Test of Phonological Processing* (5 years – 24 years 11 mths)

This American test contains many subtests and covers a wide age range. Only those appropriate for older students would be used in this context such as **Elision** (phoneme deletion), the four **Rapid Naming** and the **Verbal Memory** subtests.

N.B. The mean on the subtests is 10 and the standard deviation is 3. Therefore a score of 7 is **'low average'**; 6 or less **'below average'**.

- *Digit Memory Test (6 – adult)*[24]

Research has shown that deficits in **verbal memory** (the phonological loop of working memory) are almost universal in dyslexia. Should scores on digits **backwards** be markedly lower than **forwards** (more than 2 less) this may indicate a particular difficulty in 'working memory'.

Visual/motor skills

The impetus to assess **visual/motor skills** may well come from concerns about handwriting legibility and speed at this stage.

- **VMI** *Beery-Buktenica Developmental Test of Visual-Motor Integration 5th edition* (2 – 18 years)

- *The Morrisby Manual Dexterity Test* (15+)

A useful test (quick to administer and cheap to buy!) for demonstrating significant problems with fine motor skills.

- **SDMT** *Symbol Digit Modalities Test* (8 – 17 years)

Also quick to administer, it measures facility with printed symbols and visual-motor speed

The tests referred to above are not the only ones that can be used. Others exist, more are being and will be developed. The pattern of difficulties presented by some candidates will mean that the proper course of action is to refer him on to a practitioner with different skills and resources. An important aspect of responsible professional practice is recognition of the limits of one's own area of expertise.

General ability

Since 'appropriate entry' is the Centre's responsibility and will to a large extent depend on each candidate's teacher's assessment of attainment in that subject, assessment of general ability is not generally needed in this context. There are always cases, however, where either the Centre – or very often the candidate – has a 'need to know' when considering his suitability for a particular level of study.

Assessment of general ability is fully discussed in Backhouse & Morris 2005[25] and Specialist Teachers will be familiar with some if not all of the following resources:

---

[24] Free to download from the Dyslexia Action website:
http://www.dyslexiaaction.org.uk/Administration/uploads/digit.pdf
[25] Backhouse G and Morris K 2005 **Dyslexia? Assessing and Reporting, the Patoss Guide** London, Hodder Murray

- **BPVS II** *British Picture Vocabulary Test, Second Edition* (3 – 15 years 8 months)

A useful resource since norms for students whose first language is not English are available, which may be helpful when considering the need for a bilingual dictionary. However, most GCSE candidates will be near to the ceiling of this test. Therefore alternative resources (see below) may be preferable.

- *Peabody Picture Vocabulary Test: Third edition* (2 years 6 months – 90+)

Quick to administer (11 – 12 minutes) this wide age range resource measures receptive vocabulary for standard English and provides an indicator of verbal ability. Two parallel forms are provided.

- *Ravens Progressive Matrices and Vocabulary scales* (7 – 18 years)

A re-standardisation study using the SPM-Plus: Standard Progressive Matrices-Plus and MHV: Mill Hill Vocabulary Scale has been completed. The resource has been redesigned, simplified and updated and will be available in January 2008.

- **NNAT** *Naglieri Nonverbal Ability Test* (5 – 17 years)

Stemming from the older Matrix Analogies Test, this is a useful resource in FE or with students who have language difficulties or EAL. Administration time is 30 minutes.

The results of tests such as **CAT** *Cognitive Abilities Test* (non-verbal result only) may already be available in school, or *Morrisby Profile* (CST & GAT-P sub-tests) following a Careers Guidance assessment.

- **WRIT** *Wide Range Intelligence Test (4 – 84 years)*

Available to Specialist Teachers in the UK, the WRIT contains four sub-tests which measure verbal and visual abilities. The scores can be aggregated to give a general ability measure.

It should be remembered that studies have generally shown relatively low correlations of 0.4 to 0.6 between IQ test results and exam grades; so we should never underestimate the contribution that good teaching and hard work can make to educational attainment, nor overestimate the significance of IQ/ability scores!

Completion of Form 8 JCQ/AA/LD

Please remember to **only** give the information requested in Section C 1, 2, 3 & 4 and put all other relevant facts under **Other relevant information.** This makes it easier for AB staff to process the forms.

For example, many people are unsure about how to comment on reading speed (Section C, 2) if they use the Edinburgh 4 or WRAT-E. No standard score is obtained nor speed in words per minute from these tests although both are timed. It is not, however, compulsory to complete every entry – only those which are relevant. A pupil who reads extremely slowly, when completing either test, would inevitably obtain an extremely low score for **Comprehension** – simply because he did not finish. The question then is: which seems the most appropriate access arrangement – a reader, or extra time? Any help you can give the Centre on this matter as a result of your assessment results (which may include other diagnostic reading tests), observations & discussion with the candidate, should be set out under **Other Relevant Information.** It is then up to Centre staff to make the decision.

Finalising your report for the Centre

1. Carefully check your marking and standard scores.

2. Check you have all necessary information regarding candidate's case history, history of provision and normal way of working.

3. Complete your pro-forma summarising all the evidence [see pp 66 & 67].

4. Complete Form 8, Section C if appropriate.

5. Proofread your report.

6. Discuss findings with SENCO / ALS Manager.

Student Record Sheet, Access Arrangements GCSE etc

Name of Candidate:		DoB:	Year of Entry:
Date of Assessment:		Chron. Age:	Candidate Number:

Section A, History of Need		Section C, Profile of LDs		

		Reading Skills		
History of difficulties				
Level on CoP		**1. Reading Accuracy**		

KS 3 NCT scores:	E	M	Sc	Name of test	
				Test ceiling	
Previous Assessment? Y/N	By whom?			Date of admin	
				S.Score	

Screening Tests		Reading age	
Name of test	Score	Comments	

		2. Reading Speed & Comprehension		
		Name of test		
		Test ceiling		
Learning Support?		Date of admin		
		Speed wpm		
Previous Access Arrangements? (Date & Exam)		Speed S.S.?		
		Compreh S.S.	Set time	ET
		Comments		
Normal way of working:		Writing Skills		
		3. Spelling assessment		

National Curriculum Levels		Name of test	
Subject:	Level:	Test ceiling	
		Date of admin	
		S.Score	
		% unrec words	
		Comments	
		4. Writing Speed	
		Free wr, wpm	
		% unrec words	
		Dict/WP wpm	
		Quality of lang	
		Other relevant info	

Section B, Recommendations

1	
2	
3	

Student's comments:

Caroline Read 2007.   This sheet can be photocopied without infringing copyright.

Table for comparing results on standardised tests

Student's Name…………………………………….

Date tested…………….

Assessed by …………………………………….

Standard Deviation =	-3	-2	-1	0	+1	+2	+3
Standardised scores =	55	70	85	100	114	115	130
Test	Well Below	Below average	← Average range →			Above average	Well Above

This sheet can be photocopied without infringing copyright.

9. Basic Concepts in Psychometrics

In this section, you will find a brief summary of some of the most important issues you must understand when choosing, using, scoring and interpreting the results of standardised tests in an educational setting.[26]

There are two main types of standardised test:

1) maximum performance – where the testee has to do the best he can, e.g. single word reading tests.

2) typical performance tests – which assess how the testee generally behaves, thinks, feels, etc., such as questionnaires.

For assessment of learning difficulties tests of maximum performance are usually used.

Choosing standardised tests

Test manuals vary regarding the amount of technical information they give. The contents range from basic facts to a large amount of complex statistical information, generated during the test development and standardisation. The amount of work involved in gathering this data is very considerable and the reason why tests are expensive.

> N.B. You should be very wary of tests developed by individuals or small organisations that may not have the financial resources or expertise to support the proper development of tests.

The standardisation sample

Every time we look up an individual's test results in norm tables, we are in effect comparing his performance with that of the group used during the test development and standardisation. The larger that group and more widely distributed across different areas (inner city, suburban, rural, etc.) the more likely it is that the statistics regarding what is average, above and below, are meaningful and 'true' for the population as a whole.

A reading test, for example, developed and standardised in grammar schools in one of the counties that still retains the 11+ will probably produce a different value for 'average' from one developed in non-selective schools in one of our more deprived inner cities.

Furthermore, since language, literacy standards and other attributes within both school and general population are constantly evolving; norms established several decades ago may not be fair representations of the population now.

The use of equating techniques where testees take a new test and a recognised standardised one is a powerful method of linking or equating standards and gaining reliable information using smaller samples of students.

> **Action:**
> Choose tests which have been recently standardised on, or equated to, a large, nationally representative sample.

---

[26] Reproduced from Backhouse G and Morris K 2005 **Dyslexia? Assessing and Reporting, the Patoss Guide** London, Hodder Murray

The **age-range** of the standardisation sample is also extremely important – particularly during the primary school age when development of skills and knowledge is much faster than later on. This is why tests usually provide separate norm tables for each 6 months during the early school years, then expand the age groups to 1 year in the secondary phase and as abilities 'plateau' in adulthood they are given 5 or 10 year bands thereafter. Norms for 7 year olds will not be appropriate for most 6 or 8 year olds, but those for 16 year olds may not be too far from the mark for 25 year olds (but see below re. Age Equivalent scores).

For statistical reasons, tests do not discriminate well at the extremes of their age range and so best practice is to use tests for individuals whose ages are well within the test 'ceiling' and 'floor'.

> **Action:**
> Choose a test which more than covers the age range of the students you are assessing.

Reliability

The reliability of a test reflects the extent to which it consistently measures the target skill(s). There are many ways of assessing reliability, each with its own advantages and so reliability is not a fixed quantity. You will find details of the methods used in the test manual. Important aspects are:

Test-re-test reliability: Testees should obtain the same scores if they take the test on 2 separate occasions. This is an important issue where there are parallel forms.

> N.B. In the assessment context, retesting within a short period of time is likely to produce a higher result due to learning that occurred during the first trial and so is not recommended. (During the standardisation process this is accounted for.)

Administrator/Interscorer reliability: The same results should be obtained no matter who is administering or marking the test.

Data about the **internal reliability** of a test is usually represented by reliability coefficients. The **reliability coefficient (r)** indicates what proportion of the test variance is due to 'real' individual differences. E.g. if r = 0.87, that means 87% of the variance is 'true' and 13% is likely to be due to sampling error. The higher the reliability coefficient of a test (up to 1.0 = perfect reliability), the more confidence may be placed in the consistency and precision of the results it generates. Look for values above 0.8 and preferably above 0.9. The lower the reliability, the less confidence you can have concerning the testee's real ability, based on that particular test result.

An often-quoted measure of internal reliability is known as Cronbach's alpha. This checks to see what proportion of the testees get questions of differing difficulty correct. For example only the best should get the hardest ones correct. Values over 0.8 indicate well-designed and balanced tests that should enable differentiation to occur.

When all the items in a test are 'operating' i.e. not too difficult or too easy then the more items there are in a test, the greater its reliability. Therefore the results of short tests – in terms of number of items – should never be relied upon in a formal assessment, without a great deal of complementary and supporting evidence.

> N.B. A test such as the TOWRE[27] may be short in terms of time taken – because it is a speed test. However, the number of items to be read in 45 seconds. is high, as are the reliability coefficients.

[27] Test of Word Reading Efficiency

A number of computer based tests now screen individuals to ensure they only do questions of appropriate level difficulty. This has the advantage of not wasting time and effort on too easy or too hard questions and still maintains reliability. The minimum number of items in a multiple-choice test should be 30, pitched at around the appropriate level.

> **Action**
> Choose tests with high reliability coefficients and a goodly number of items to be tackled by the testee.

Confidence bands and standard error of measurement

Some test manuals provide data regarding standard errors of measurement (SEM) and confidence bands/intervals – either in the norm tables (e.g. NARA II[28]) or in the chapter about test reliability (e.g. CTOPP[29]).

Standard errors of measurement (SEM) provide a 'ring of confidence' around a particular test score, since there is always the possibility of a discrepancy between a person's 'true' and obtained score. (Psychological testing is not an exact science!) The SEM is the likely size of this discrepancy and confidence intervals are based on SEMs. They are usually defined thus:

it is 68% certain that a person's 'true' score will be within the band of scores lying 1SEM either side of his obtained score:

it is 95% certain that it will be within plus/minus 2 SEMs of his obtained score;

it is 99% certain for the range 3 SEMs either side.

There is an inverse relationship between the reliability coefficient of a test and its SEM. A highly reliable test will have a small SEM and so each obtained score is likely to be close to the hypothetically 'true' one.

Validity

Validity studies tell you to what extent the test measures what it says it does and has to be considered in the context of what the test user needs to know. Again, there are different ways of measuring validity because there are different aspects. The main ones are:

Concurrent validity shows that people who are known to differ on the task being measured, obtain correspondingly low – average – high scores on the test.

> e.g. Do good and bad clerks score well and poorly on clerical aptitude tests?

Predictive validity can be used to tell what will happen in the future.

> e.g. Do IQ tests predict exam grades?

Content validity relates to the how well the test covers all relevant aspects of the skills being measured.

> e.g. Does an untimed single word reading test measure 'real' reading ability – the capacity to read text with full comprehension straight away?

> **Action:**
> Choose a test which focuses on and measures the precise skills you wish to investigate. Select tests that provide sound evidence of their validity for the purpose.

---

[28] NARAII Neale Analysis of Reading Ability; second revised British edition
[29] CTOPP Comprehensive Test of Phonological Processing

Much information regarding validity (as well as reliability) is expressed in terms of correlations with results of other similar tests, exam results, teachers' ratings, studies with special groups and so on.

Correlation coefficients

Correlation coefficients express the relationship between two variables, but do NOT necessarily mean that one causes the other – although it may.

For example, there is a very high correlation between children's reading ability and the size of their feet – they both increase with age (the underlying factor), but neither causes the other!

Coefficients vary between minus one (perfect negative correlation) through zero (absence of correlation) to plus one (perfect correlation). So when a coefficient is less than one, one measure is influenced by some factor not found in the other.

If you multiply the decimal by 10, then square the result, an estimated percentage is obtained of the proportion of the two measures that represent a common factor.

As an example, let us consider the relationship between reading ability and verbal IQ.

> The NARA II manual shows that the correlation between verbal ability – as measured by the BAS II[30] and reading comprehension – as measured by the NARA II is 0.65. So we can say that 42% (6.5 x 6.5) of what is measured by the 2 tests is common, but a host of factors other than those measured by IQ tests (e.g. literacy, motivation, quality of teaching etc.) are also highly relevant. However, the same table shows the correlation between verbal ability and rate of reading is lower – 0.47, which means that only 22% of these 2 indices represents a common factor.

Looking at these concepts in another way … if everyone who passes test X always passes test Y, then they are a perfectly correlated pair and X has a 100% accurate predictive validity for Y.

Significance and Probability

Against all this data about correlations – both in test manuals and research reports, you will find information about the significance of the results given as Probability coefficients (p) or significance. These tell you about the likelihood of getting a particular result, or set of results, by chance. The smaller p is, (e.g. 0.05, 0.01, 0.001) the more significant the result; i.e. it would have been very unlikely to have occurred by chance.

Using standardised tests

A principal characteristic of standardised tests is that the administration procedure, stimulus materials and scoring are prescribed and exactly the same for all who use and take them and match the method in which the test was standardised. Since all testees have (as near as possible) the same experience, differences in scores should reflect true differences in ability.

Action:
Make sure that you know and follow the procedures for administration of any test that you use. The manual will usually tell you the exact words to use and whether (for example) you may repeat a question.

---

[30] British Ability Scales 2nd edition

Understanding Scores and Interpretation of Results

Most tests of ability and attainment, if administered to a large, representative sample of the population, produce roughly bell-shaped (normal) distributions, with lots of people scoring in the middle/average range (the 'central tendency') and far fewer having extreme (very high or very low) results.

The scales are usually converted so that every test has the same **normal probability curve** – a smooth symmetrical frequency curve having known mathematical properties.

Raw scores (direct numerical reports of performance, e.g. 60/100 on a test) are converted to **derived scores** – showing each person's relative position, compared to his peers, by using norm tables. There are 3 types of **derived scores**: Standard; Percentiles; and Age Equivalent.

Standard or Standardised scores

These show the testee's position relative to the mean for his age group, using the **standard deviation** as the unit of measurement.

The mean is the arithmetical average score for the reference group.

> (Other measures of 'central tendency' are median and mode. The median is the middle score and the mode is the most frequently occurring score in a particular set. These can be useful in situations where the distribution of scores is heavily skewed, or the mean is misleading because a few 'outlier' results are very different from the others.)

The standard deviation (SD) is the average deviation from the mean – regardless of direction. Scores within 1 SD either side of the mean on any test are classified as 'average' (sometimes sub-divided into 'lower' and 'higher').

If a **normal distribution** is 'sliced' into vertical bands 1 SD wide, a fixed percentage of cases **always** falls into each band and the overwhelming majority will fall within 3 SDs either side of the mean. The largest proportion of individual scores are 'bunched up' in the middle band (1 SD either side of the mean).

Approximately two thirds (68%) of individuals will fall in the 'average' range, defined in this way (34% either side of the mean). See Fig. 9.1, below.

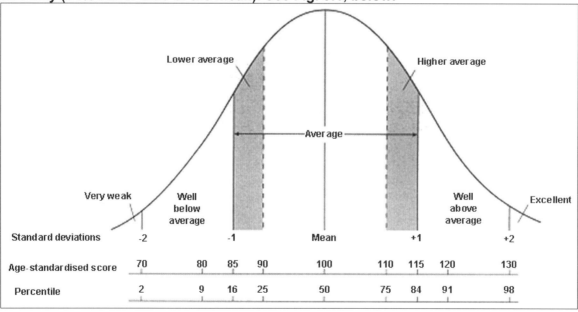

Fig. 9.1 The Normal Distribution Curve/SDs & percentiles. [34]

Norms tell you what the normal range of performance is, for a particular age range/group (e.g. 7 year olds, computer programmers etc.)

Norm referenced testing may be used for individual assessment (see **ipsative testing** below) or screening – to establish which members of a group (class) have abilities or attainments below a certain level, in order to trigger further assessment, learning support etc., or special arrangements during examinations. The bench mark used for provision of LS may vary between organisations such as schools and Local Authorities, according to their resources and may be for instance 2 or 2½ SDs below the mean.

Standard scores are the most appropriate type of derived score to use when considering a testee's results. They indicate how far away from the average level an individual is in terms of actual performance on a test. Furthermore, by measuring this distance in terms of standard deviation units, we can compare an individual's performance on one test with his results on another and derive a profile of strengths and weaknesses – as well as see how well he matches up to his peers.

Percentile scores

These reflect the percentage of the group whose scores fall below that of the testee. A 10th percentile rank is therefore a low result (90% would do better) and a 90th (per)centile rank is pretty good as only 10% would exceed this score.

There is relatively **little difference** between the **raw** scores of a large **percentage** of individuals whose results are near the mean. Thus **percentile** scores between 17 & 83 are technically 'within the average range'.

Percentile scores magnify small differences near the mean which may not be significant; and reduce the apparent size of large differences near the tails of the curve i.e. the difference, in terms of actual performance, between percentile ranks of 5 & 15 is far larger than that between percentile ranks of 40 & 50 (see **Hypothetical example**, Fig. 9.2 overleaf). Normalised **standard scores** avoid this since the intervals on a standardised scale are all equal – but they are not generally well-understood by non-specialists!

See the example in figure 9.2.

[31] Diagnostic Reading Analysis, Manual 2004, Crumpler M and McCarty C, Hodder Murray, 7 – 16 years.

Hypothetical example

Say we measured 1000 adult women and found their average height to be 5 ft. 5 ins.

How would we then define **below average** (short) and **above average** (tall), and how many women might be expected to fall into these categories?

This is where the standard deviation is useful since it is a measure of the **variance**, in relation to the **mean** and is a generic mechanism for defining the above and below average 'benchmarks' on any standardized scale.

By finding the deviation (difference) from the mean of all 1000 women:
(e.g. if height   = 5 ft. 2 then deviation from mean = 3 ins.
..   ..   = 5 ft. 7   ..   ..   ..   = 2 ins
..   ..   = 5 ft. 5   ..   ..   ..   = 0 ins
                                      & etc.)

- the **standard deviation** can be calculated by applying a set formula to the results obtained from the sample. Let us suppose the SD turned out to be 2 inches.

We can now define (statistically) the average range as between 5 ft. 3 ins. and 5 ft. 7 ins. and expect roughly 680 out of every 1000 women (68%) to fall between these limits. We can also define what we mean by above and below average in terms of height and using the SD (of 2 ins.) can predict that only 20 women are likely to be under 5ft. 1 in. and another 20 above 5 ft. 9 (2 SDs above & below the mean) using our knowledge of percentiles.

Mean =	5 ft. 5 ins
Standard deviation	2 ins.
Above average (+1 SD)	5 ft. 7 ins. (16% of popn.)
Below average (-1SD)	5 ft. 3 ins. (16% of popn.)
Well Above average (+2 SDs)	5 ft. 9 ins. (2% of popn.)
Well Below average (-2SDs)	5 ft. 1 ins. (2% of popn.)

As for percentiles – it is now relatively easy to see why they can be misleading. Out of our 680 average height women many are likely to be almost or exactly 5ft 5ins. It is clearly a nonsense to call someone who is 5ft. 4½ short, or another of 5ft. 5½ tall. You would be hard pressed to notice the difference between them and might easily misjudge who was the taller, even though one might be at the 35th percentile (5ft. 4½) and the other at the 65th (5ft. 5½). This sounds like a huge difference – but in terms of 'raw scores' is in fact negligible in relation either to each other, or to the mean.

If, however, we think in terms of SD units (of 2 ins.) we can say one is taller than the other if there is at least 2 ins. between them; or one is below average if she is 5ft. 3 or under.

Figure 9.2 Hypothetical example

The language used to describe scores

Different test publishers use a variety of verbal labels such as 'low average'; 'superior' and so forth to describe different sections of the normal curve, which can be confusing. By far the safest and most meaningful thing to do is to stick to the correct statistical divisions based on standard deviations.

The difference between 'below average' and a 'deficit'

Would it be reasonable to say that women measuring 5ft. 3ins. have a problem? Clearly not! However, being 5ft. 2 (1.5 SDs below the mean – in the '**moderate deficit**' range), may begin to affect life on the odd occasion. One's vision is restricted in crowds, choice of some clothes restricted to those available in 'Petite sizes' and it's hard to reach things off higher shelves – nothing serious, but a nuisance at times. At 2 SDs or more below the mean (**severe deficit**), 5ft. 1 and below in this hypothetical example, more everyday things may become difficult – standard kitchen equipment is uncomfortably high and some careers – where there are minimum height requirements – are barred.

It remains to be said that 'deficits' are defined in relation to the demands made on the ability/characteristic measured. Height, for example, is only an issue in certain situations.

So long as we know the **mean** and **standard deviation** of any **standardised scale**, we can interpret a student's performance in relation to others in his age group, also his own score on other tests. For both purposes, it will lead to sounder conclusions if standard deviation units, rather than percentile scores are used. Some common standard score systems are given in the table, but in the UK most tests now report a derived score using a mean of 100 and this is often called a quotient:

	Mean	Standard Deviation
Stanines (e.g. NARA, CAT[32] tests)	5	2
T-scores (e.g. BAS)	50	10
Deviation Quotients (e.g. WISC[33] IQ & Index scores; PhAB[34], BPVS[35])	100	15
Wechsler IQ & CTOPP subtests	10	3

Age Equivalent scores

The third type of derived score is the **Age Equivalent** or **Test Age**. This tells you the chronological age, or age range, for which an individual's raw score is average.

However, **Age Equivalents** become less and less appropriate as the age of the testee increases, since the rate of development of skills and attainments slows.

This is illustrated in the table overleaf concerning two pairs of learners.

> A difference of 1 word read on the TOWRE (Sight Word Efficiency) by the two 7 year olds only alters the **Age Equivalents** by 3 months. The Standard Scores are within the average range for both and the **Age Equivalents** reflect this.

> Contrast this with the 24 year old reading just 2 less words than the 16 year old. The **Age Equivalents** are roughly the same for both learners, but the 24 year old's looks horribly low, some 9 years below his chronological age. However his Standard Score is actually within the average range for his age group (as it is for the younger student), because the norms at 16 are remarkably similar to those at 24. In fact the TOWRE 'collapses' the entire group between 17.0 and 24-11 years into 1 table, whereas the 6 to 8 year. olds (where development is very fast) have a different norm table for every 6 months.

[32] Cognitive Ability Tests
[33] Wechsler Intelligence Scale for Children
[34] Phonological Ability Battery
[35] British Picture Vocabulary Scales

Chronological Age	Raw score	Standard score	Age Equivalent
7 yrs. 0 mths.	31	98	7 yrs. 3 mths.
7 yrs. 6 mths.	30	91	7 yrs. 0 mths.

16 yrs. 6 mths.	92	98	16 yrs. 0 mths.
24 yrs. 6 mths	90	91	15 yrs. 6 mths.

A good rule of thumb is to avoid using **Test Age** scores altogether if possible, but especially for testees in the secondary and adult age range. If, for some reason, **Age Equivalents** are required for someone in this older age group, you should take care to explain any large discrepancies between test age and chronological age.

Furthermore, you **must not** quote standardised scores if you have assessed a learner whose chronological age is higher than the test 'ceiling' (e.g. the BPVS with a 23 year-old). In such cases you can only give qualitative descriptions of his performance in the report such as *well-developed* etc.

Ipsative testing

This term is used when a profile of individual strengths and weaknesses is based on a person's scores on different tests. Conclusions about his differential abilities, learning difficulties, attainments and so-on are often drawn on the basis of contrasts of **one or more standard deviations** between standardised scores on different tests.

(Although it is generally acceptable to compare standard scores from different tests caution should be exercised if the two tests were standardised on very different populations or at different times (e.g. 1970 cf 1990 – a generation apart).

Discrepancies in a learner's profile are a key factor in assessment but we must be careful to distinguish between deficit and discrepancy. Few people perform at the same level in every test administered to them. One person may get well above average marks on a verbal test and an average score for non-verbal reasoning. He is likely to find language-based subjects easier than practical ones. The difference of 2 SDs between scores is highly meaningful regarding his potential strengths and weaknesses. But since the lower score is not in the *deficit* range, it cannot be said that he has a learning difficulty! He may well have a problem, however, if he chooses to study technical or scientific subjects at advanced levels.

'Lower average' and 'higher average' scores

It is often the case that certain test scores are not quite in the *below average* range and yet all the evidence from the case history, our observations and other tests convinces us that there are sufficient grounds for diagnosing a learning difficulty. Given the degree of error inherent in tests it is sometimes justifiable to base conclusions on scores falling within the narrow 'slice', just within the outer edges of the average range, called *lower average* and *higher average* as shown in Fig.9.1, page 72.

10. Case Studies

The case studies which follow are all from 'real life'. Permission to use the details given has in all cases been given, although names have been changed. These examples have been chosen to demonstrate a range of needs and illustrate the process of gathering the evidence required before appropriate decisions can be made about access arrangements. Further examples are given in the JCQ Regulations booklet which is **the primary reference**.

Please note that the first two candidates – John and Shelley – were assessed in 2003 and 2004 and the regulations have changed since then. John for example, would now be permitted a scribe in his English exam. This makes the point that the regulations do **change** from year to year and you must make sure that you are always in possession of the correct edition of the JCQ handbook.

Photocopiable resources

The pro-forma for summarising candidate information mentioned in Chapter 8 are used with these case studies and a blank is included on page 66, as well as a blank chart for comparing standardised test results to aid analysis of results, page 67. Both may be photocopied for your own use, but are *not* official forms and should *not* be sent to an Awarding Body!

Case Study 1   JOHN

This boy in Y10 was referred for assessment right at the beginning of his GCSE course. John was an able and high-achieving pupil at a selective grammar school and staff had no doubts about his potential to achieve 9 good grades if appropriate access arrangements were agreed by the ABs. He had severe DCD (Developmental Co-ordination Disorder) which was first diagnosed when he was in Y4. He had 2 EP reports on file. He was on the SEN register throughout his primary schooling and since secondary transfer, due to his extreme difficulties with writing. He was supported in English, History and RE by Teaching Assistants. He could type but extremely slowly and used a laptop in other subjects for copying and making notes as best he could. Teachers scribed for him during all tests and exams in school and his parents for homework. He is quite used to dictating his work which he did fluently. The SENCO needed a specialist report to support an application for him to use a scribe for all his GCSE exams.

At the assessment session, John mentioned that he had a long history of trouble with his vision and found reading tiring. His reading was therefore assessed as well as his writing. His test results (see Fig. 10.1.2) showed that his accuracy at word-level was excellent but not his speed. His results on the TOWRE were below average. His reading comprehension was average, but given 25% extra time he was able to finish the Edinburgh 4 and improve his score by a full standard deviation. It was therefore concluded that he had a specific difficulty with reading speed and an additional time allowance was suggested.

John's writing skills were assessed in various ways with the possible adjustments in mind (extra time / transcript / word-processor / scribe). His spelling – as can be seen from the sample of word-processed writing – is good enough for him to communicate effectively in this way. However, he types extremely slowly (2 SDs below the average handwriting speed for Y10) and was visibly tired at the end of the 20 minute trial. His handwriting (see Figure 10.1.1, below) is truly 'incomprehensible' and his distress when asked to produce a sample was evident. He had no difficulty continuing on the same topic of 'Rowing' when demonstrating his ability to dictate fluently (although he did not know the assessor).

WRITING SAMPLES

Free-writing: hand-written; 10 mins. 7 wpm.

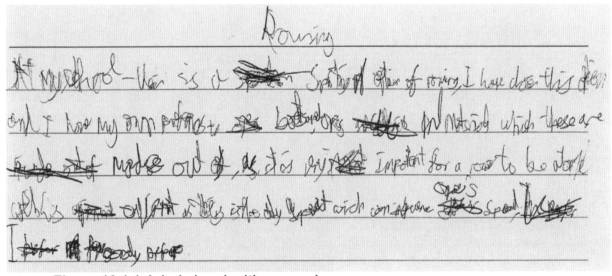

Figure 10.1.1 John's handwriting sample

Free-writing: Dictated : 7 mins.; 25 wpm.

Rowing (cont.)

Personally I prefer carbon-fibre oars, in a wooden quad, which is a boat which consists of 4 people. The reason why I prefer this is that carbon fibre oars are light and easily manoeuvrable and a wooden boat is much more sturdy than a carbon fibre one. I prefer teams of four in a boat as this amount of people requires very little technique (which I am poor at performing). I also have my own preferences for formal races. I enjoy racing on a narrow river with lots of turns during a regatta, which is a race on the water where all the boats start at the same time, as opposed to a head race which is a time trial and everyone starts at different times. The reason why I prefer regattas is that it creates more of a sense of atmosphere which creates adrenaline because one can see one's opponents and is racing against their physical presence rather than imagined opponents – as is the case in a head race.

Free-writing: Word-processed: 20 mins.; 5 wpm.

Music

In this day and age the music industry controls much of the nashon's youth's ways of life and gives anyone an unforgiving overall impreshion of people's personalitys, which I feel is one of the problems with modern music. My favrite type of music is rock, this is not only because I prefer the types of sounds which constucts the music but I also prefer the culture which surronds rock, as oposed to the thug-like culture which surronds music such as garage. Music and culture have become unseperbly linked together part of the problem with this link is that one can no longer just deside which (*sounds they prefer*) **

*** During 5 minutes (i.e. 25%) additional time allowance John added just 3 words.*

Standard Deviation =	-3	-2	-1 0 +1	+2	+3
Standardised scores =	55	70	85 100 114	115	130
Test	Well Below	Below average	← *Average range* →	Above average	Well Above
Reading – Accuracy					
SW reading – WRAT (untimed)			114		
SW reading – TOWRE (timed)		78			
Nonword reading – TOWRE (timed)		79			
Reading – Speed & Comprehension					
Edinburgh 4			97		
Edinburgh 4 + 25% extra time			112		
Writing: Accuracy & legibility					
Spelling (printed) – WRAT		84			
Percentage unrecognisable – 25%					
Free-writing speed:					
– handwriting		7 wpm			
%age unrecognisable – 50%+					
– dictated				25 wpm	
– word-processed		5 wpm			

Fig. 10.1.2 John's test results

Discussion

The assessment evidence supported the Centre's view that the most appropriate access arrangement for John was a scribe whenever possible. His word-processing skills were simply too slow for this to be an option for all his papers. An extra 50% time was requested plus use of a word processor in papers where a scribe is not permitted. The Centre had not foreseen one difficulty, however, which concerned his course work. If he stayed after school to work and dictate to a teacher, he missed the school bus. His parents could not scribe course work to be assessed. The solution was for John to use a Dictaphone and hand the tape to a Teaching Assistant the next day. She would type up his work and send it back to him as an e-mail attachment so that he could edit and continue with his projects.

He was strongly advised by the assessor to learn how to use voice-activated word-processing in order to become more independent as soon as possible. The Centre also decided to allow John extra time to compensate for his slow reading and visual discomfort.

Examples of entries on Form 8 JCQ/AA/LD

Section A

History of Need

John experienced severe difficulty and delay with the acquisition of literacy skills. EP reports in Y4 & Y 7 detailed a well above average IQ, but very weak visuo-motor skills/severe dyspraxia (DCD). He now reads well, but is unable to produce legible handwriting. He knows how to use a computer but types too slowly for most purposes. With the aid of a scribe he achieved above average results in KS3 SATs. He is well-behaved & highly motivated to succeed.

History of Provision

From Y7 – 8 John had in-class support for written work and training in keyboard skills. Since Y8 he uses a laptop in class but a scribe in tests and examinations. We are confident that with the requested access arrangements he will gain good grades at GCSE.

Section C

Other relevant information

John's handwriting is completely illegible. He can type moderately accurately as regards spelling, but very slowly and becomes fatigued and distressed. He dictates fluently.

John has a specific difficulty with reading **speed**, although his accuracy and comprehension are age-appropriate. His results on timed tests of both word & nonword reading were below average (SS of 78 & 79).

Outcome

The ABs all agreed to the Centre's request for a scribe[36]; 50% extra time and use of a word-processor for English. John achieved one A*, 5 As (for arts / language-based subjects) and 3 Bs for Science and Maths in the GCSE.

---

[36] Under current JCQ regulations, John would be permitted a scribe in the English exam.

He then went on to study History, Classics & Religious Studies at A level. He was allowed a scribe for course-work. Despite several attempts with the latest voice-activated word-processing software, John did not find that this technology worked for him. His lack of fluency when composing – as he thought aloud and honed each sentence – was a significant hindrance. So an undergraduate studying IT who lived nearby was employed for 3 x 2 hour sessions a week to type for John – an experience they both enjoyed and gained from. With the support of a scribe during the examinations, John achieved an A in History and two B grades. At the time of writing he is about to go to a prestigious university to read Philosophy – and pursue his passion for rowing! He has been advised to try using predictive / adaptive word processing software since voice-activated has proved unsuccessful for him.

When questioned about the difference access arrangements had made to John's life so far, his Mother was forthright in her opinion that the Y10 assessment had been 'a turning point'. With that report, the school had stopped saying 'He knows more history than anyone else – but he'll never pass an exam' and set all the necessary arrangements in place. John's self-esteem and confidence in himself blossomed as his acute anxiety and frustration faded and he has not looked back since.

Case Study 2   SHELLEY

A part-time student at an Adult Education College, Shelley was referred for assessment by her English tutor. She was a qualified Nursery Nurse and had achieved NVQ 2 & 3 qualifications with literacy support. She had attended Basic Skills classes for 3 years and was now working towards a GCSE in English which she needed to further her career. Her tutor had become concerned as although Shelley was *'extremely conscientious'* and was improving all the time, she clearly had significant difficulties with spelling and speed of reading and writing. The tutor has started to think Shelley may be dyslexic and need extra time in her exams.

Shelley had never been assessed before. Her schooling was frequently interrupted due to her mother's long-term illness. She received very little learning support although she was late learning to speak, read and spell and found it very difficult to study and write essays when older. She did not have access to a computer and could not type.

As she talked about her ambitions and problems during the assessment session, Shelley's tendency to make speech errors was noticed. Her reading accuracy at word level was below average (WRAT3). Her nonword decoding was particularly weak, but sight word reading markedly better (TOWRE), although still below average. She tackled the timed reading comprehension test (WRAT-E) confidently saying that her only problem with reading was that it took her a long time. When offered extra time to finish the test, however, Shelley refused to do so saying that it was getting too hard.

Shelley's spelling was below average (WRAT3). She made logical and recognisable attempts at common words but when asked to spell words she did not know her attempts were dysphonetic (e.g. ianzliset/anxiety; reconsie/recognize). Her free-writing – although slow – was clear and legible. She used words she felt confident about and mistakes were minor. Her written style was simple but well-expressed and structured.

Cognitive tests revealed below average phonological processing skills – including rapid naming (not dependent on literacy levels) but normal IQ. The assessor was in no doubt that Shelley was dyslexic.

Shelley's normal way of working was by herself, but slowly. She could read by herself and write legibly. She had no desire to be 'helped' in any way and wanted to be assessed 'properly'. She felt it would be fair if she had extra time and was pleased to find out about the 'Read Aloud' option which she felt would be helpful and not be 'cheating'.

Outcome

The Centre arranged for her to sit her exam in a separate room to enable her to 'Read Aloud' and allowed her 25% extra time.

Shelley achieved a Grade C in GCSE English.

Standard Deviation =	-3	-2	-1 0 +1	+2	+3
Standardised scores =	*55*	*70*	85 100 114	*115*	*130*
Test	Well Below	Below average	← *Average range* →	Above average	Well Above
Reading Accuracy					
SW reading – WRAT (untimed)	67				
SW reading – TOWRE (timed)		76			
Nonword reading – TOWRE (timed)	55				
Reading Speed & Comprehension					
WRAT-E (Form G)			87		
Writing Accuracy & legibility					
Spelling – WRAT		82			
Percentage unrecognisable – 20%					
Free-writing speed					
– handwriting			11 wpm		
%age unrecognisable – 0%					
Cognitive skills					
CTOPP –Rapid Naming: Letters		5			
Digits		5			
Objects	4				
Colours			10		
Spoonerisms	< 68				
Digit Span		75			
General Ability					
WRIT – Verbal			93		
– Non-Verbal			86		

Fig. 10.2.1 Shelley's test results

Case Study 3 EMMA

by Caroline Read

Emma was referred for assessment to support an application for both reader and scribe during her GCSE courses and exams. She has a Statement of SEN due to moderate learning difficulties. She has received small group support on a daily basis since Y2 and was statemented in Y5. Weekly support from the Local Authority learning support team was then provided which continued until Y9. Emma works within a small low ability group with a teaching assistant available to help with reading, writing and comprehension as necessary. The school's SENCO comments that Emma has significant difficulties in both expressive and receptive language and finds it difficult to remember and follow instructions.

She was working below the level of the tests for Key Stage 3 National Curriculum English Tests, so took part in Teacher Assessment only. Her results were: 2c for writing, 2a for reading, and 2 for spelling. She was absent on the days of the maths tests, but scored at level 4 on the science tests. She was allowed a reader, scribe and additional time (which did not have to be applied for because of her statement). She did not use the additional time allocated in the science test, but made good use of the reader and writer.

Assessment

Emma's single word reading score (WRAT) was very low. She struggled to sound out and blend the sounds but was not usually able to work out the words she did not immediately recognise. This test was quite distressing for her and it was clear that the Edinburgh 4 test would be well beyond her capabilities. Her WRAT score was sufficient evidence to request a reader.

On the spelling test (Graded Word Spelling Test), some of Emma's errors were reasonable phonic approximations, but others were unrecognisable out of context, (grjah for gradual, get for guilty). She produced a free writing sample (Allcock), quite fluently but much of it was difficult to read due to handwriting, spelling and grammar difficulties. In contrast, when dictating to a scribe her speed increased to 24 wpm, and the content, though still fairly basic, was easy to understand in spite of one or two inconsistencies in the grammar.

Emma's slow word-finding was demonstrated by her performance on rapid naming tests (CTOPP) and could be used as evidence of need for additional time. However, although allowed extra time in class tests, end of year exams and National Curriculum Tests, Emma has never used it. She often completes papers well within the time allowed when she has answered all she can.

Appropriate entry

This case raises the issue of appropriate entry and the JCQ's advice that 'A candidate may still proceed with studying a particular subject, and not be entered for all or part of the assessment.' In some of her subjects, science for example, Emma is working at level 4 of the National Curriculum. In others, however, including English, she is working below the level of the exam and so Entry Level qualifications will be considered. The application form JCQ/AA/LD Form 8 included entries at GCSE for 6 subjects and Entry level for Maths and English.

After discussion with the SENCO and Emma's support teacher, it was decided to request permission for a reader, a scribe and 25% extra time when these are being used to compensate for her slow processing speed. However, in papers when these access arrangements are not available, extra time was not thought appropriate. The experience of the staff, who knew Emma well, was that she would not be able to use it.

Standard Deviation =	-3	-2	-1 0 +1	+2	+3
Standardised scores =	*55*	*70*	85 100 114	*115*	*130*
Test	Well Below	Below average	← Average range →	Above average	Well Above
Reading Accuracy					
SW reading – WRAT(untimed)	62				
Reading Speed & Comprehension					
Edinburgh N/a					
Writing Accuracy & legibility					
Spelling – Graded Word Spelling Test		72			
Percentage unrecognisable – 5%					
Free-writing speed					
Allcock, (20 min.) – handwriting			14 wpm		
%age unrecognisable – 5%					
– dictated				24 wpm	
Cognitive skills					
CTOPP –Rapid Naming: Objects		6			
Digits		6			
General Ability					
CAT Non-Verbal		72			
Verbal		70			

Fig. 10.3.1 **Emma's test results**

Examples of entries on Form 8 JCQ/AA/LD

Writing Skills

3. Accuracy & Legibility

Is the candidate's spelling accuracy in the **below average** range?
      YES

Does the candidate's spelling and/or handwriting render his or her free writing largely illegible?
      YES

Is the candidate's free writing incomprehensible?

      YES

Is the candidate proficient in the use of a word processor?
      NO

4. Does the candidate express him/herself in written form, more slowly than is average for his/her age?
      NO

Name of test	Allcock
Free writing speed (wpm)	14.2 WPM
Percentage of indecipherable words	Approx 5%, grammar is very confusing
Free writing speed (wpm) when dictated to an amanuensis/word-proceeded	24 WPM
Quality of language – please comment	Content and grammar greatly improved

Case Study 4   PETER

by Caroline Read

Peter is an able boy as his Richmond test standardised scores show. Tests taken on entry to secondary school show a score of 99 using the vocabulary test, and 123 for the use of language. However he had a considerable amount of support during primary and early secondary school, but was not given a statement until the April of Y7 when a formal diagnosis of Asperger's Syndrome was given.

He was referred for an assessment regarding his need for access arrangements during GCSE. Due to his concentration problems it was felt he needed more than the 25% additional time the Centre could permit themselves.

Assessment

Peter completed the single word reading test (WRAT) very slowly, but with great care, sounding and blending each syllable. He became frustrated when he reached his limits but his standardised score for **accuracy** was age-appropriate.

The Edinburgh Reading Test was administered but he found it very hard to concentrate and seemed to have no concept of the urgency of a timed assessment. He was then allowed to continue the test (using a different colour pen) to see if this was an effective arrangement for him. 50% extra time was given and so this part of the assessment took 1 hour & 7 minutes in all.

He was then asked to read *aloud* a 200 word passage from a previous GCSE English paper as an informal assessment of his strategies. He read once, slowly, but very accurately. When asked simple questions related to the text, he had to re-read, under his breath, twice before he was able to answer most of the questions. (This resulted in a reading speed of 55 words per minute, taking into account the need to re-read, but since this was not a nationally standardised test, the results could not be quoted on the JCQ report form.)

On the Allcock 20 minute Assessment of Writing Speed, Peter scored an overall speed of 9.4 wpm. However the analysis made possible because the student leaves two lines after each 5 minutes, is revealing. Peter wrote at 16.2 wpm for the first 5 minutes, 4.8 for the second, 7.4 for the third and 9.2 for the fourth. This is indicative of his mode of working, and his need to stop and think at some length as he works. The writing speed average for the last 15 minutes is 7.2 wpm. This is more than 1 SD below the average rate (of 16 wpm) for a student of his age, indicating the need for up to 100% extra time.

When dictating Peter spoke very slowly and stopped to think frequently. The final total after 10 minutes dictation of 18.5 wpm. was twice his hand-writing speed.

The PhAB scores outlined under '**Other relevant information**', demonstrate how slow Peter's phonological processing is. The PhAB has a ceiling of 14.11, just below his chronological age, but his scores were so extreme that this was considered to be an 'exceptional circumstance'. (Similar tests in the CTOPP, which has a ceiling of 24 years, would be more appropriate – if available.)

Standard Deviation =	-3	-2	-1 0 +1	+2	+3
Standardised scores =	55	70	85 100 114	115	130
Test	Well Below	Below average	← *Average range* →	Above average	Well Above
Reading Accuracy					
SW reading – WRAT(untimed)			103		
Reading Speed & Comprehension					
Edinburgh 4			89		
+ 50% extra time			101		
Writing Accuracy & legibility					
Spelling – Graded Word Spelling Test			105		
Percentage unrecognisable – none					
Free-writing speed					
Allcock, (20 min.) – handwriting		9.4 wpm			
%age unrecognisable – none					
– dictated			18 wpm		
Cognitive skills					
PhAB – Rapid Naming: Pictures		<85			
Digits	<69				
Fluency: Alliteration	<69				
Rhyme		<77			

Fig. 10.4.1 **Peter's test results**

Discussion

The liaison session after the assessment demonstrated the importance of the specialist discussing the needs of the candidate with those who know his normal working practice in the Centre. My initial suggestions were to apply for a prompter, extra time, (though I was unsure how much extra time), and a scribe. I felt that the slow writing speed score, which doubled when dictated, warranted a scribe.

The school felt that Peter would be able to use, and they would be able to administer, 50% extra time. However, the SENCO felt very strongly that even though his writing speed was very slow, there was a certain amount of automaticity for him in thinking and writing himself. Introduction of a scribe into the situation would require significant retraining.

The Centre was not familiar with the availability of a prompter, but since the assessment took place early in year 10 staff had time to attempt to train him to use one before the final exams.

(Use of a prompter is a **Type C** arrangement.) However, a prompter is only allowed to say the candidate's name or tap the table or the student's arm to bring them back on task, and this can need a considerable amount of training for an Aspergers student to grasp. Throughout the assessment his tendency to lose concentration was noted, or to take a very long time to think after each question was asked. Not knowing him, it was difficult for the assessor to ascertain which it was, on each occasion. He needed to be brought back to the task in hand on a number of occasions. This reinforces the wisdom of using a prompter who is familiar with the candidate and may be able to tell the difference between the two.

Peter sat his GCSE's before the arrangement of Oral Language Modifiers was introduced. Whilst he might have benefited from this help with comprehension, (only carrier language, not technical language can be rephrased) and had access to this type of support in clas (his LSA would had reworded for him if he did not understand) he would not have qualified as his reading comprehension score was in the low average, rather than below average range.

Outcome

It was therefore decided to apply for 50% extra time and provide a prompter if this proved helpful. Some uncertainty was felt as to whether the 50% extra time would be agreed since Awarding Bodies are reluctant to grant more than 25% extra time except in the most extreme cases.

However, the application for 50% extra time was agreed by all three Awarding Bodies concerned.

Peter gained the following results

English	D	**English Literature**	C
French	A	**German**	A
Science: Double Award	C & C	**Mathematics**	E
ICT	C	**Art and Design**	D

Examples of entries on Form 8 JCQ/AA/LD

Other relevant information

This candidate has almost no concept of time in an examination, and often appears to 'drift off'. He frequently does not finish a paper even when allowed 50% extra time.

His phonological processing is extremely slow. He scored below average (i.e. more than 1SD below the mean) on the rapid naming and fluency tests in the PhAB despite being a few months above the test ceiling when tested.

Due to his particular learning difficulties, a scribe is not thought an appropriate arrangement. A prompter who knows him well and can distinguish between the times when he is taking time to think, and when he has lost concentration will suit him better.

Case Study 5   DIANE

by Caroline Read

This last example will be a familiar situation in some Centres. As can be seen from the school's 'Student Record Sheet' (**Fig. 10.5.2**) Diane has an EP report dated when she was in Y7, confirming that she is dyslexic. Teachers say that her spelling is weak and she had some extra spelling tuition at school during Y8.

She now reads well and extra time made no difference to her score on the Edinburgh. She also writes quite fluently – at an age-appropriate speed. Although she makes spelling mistakes these are minor. She types much faster than she can write, but since there is no problem in reading her scripts (her spelling is logical and her handwriting legible) there is no justification for an application to use a word-processor. She does not use one in class.

The analysis of her assessment results (**Fig. 10.5.1**) showed that her literacy skills are now within the normal range for her age and she has no problems with word-finding. A small extra time allowance of 10% was agreed to compensate for any residual difficulties with spelling.

Also see sample of student record sheet (**Fig. 10.5.2**) completed for Diane overleaf.

Standard Deviation =	-3	-2	-1 0 +1	+2	+3
Standardised scores =	55	70	85 100 114	115	130
Test	Well Below	Below average	← Average range →	Above average	Well Above
Reading Accuracy					
SW reading – WRAT(untimed)			104		
Reading Speed & Comprehension					
Edinburgh 4			103		
+ extra time			104		
Writing Accuracy & legibility					
Spelling – Graded Word Spelling Test			85		
Percentage unrecognisable – none					
Free-writing speed					
Allcock, (20 min.) – handwriting			16 wpm		
%age unrecognisable – none					
– dictated					38 wpm
Cognitive skills					
CTOPP Rapid Naming: Colours			9		
Objects			8		
Letters			8		
Digits			9		

Fig. 10.5.1 Diane's test results

Name of Candidate:	Diane	DoB:	Year of Entry:
Date of Assessment: Year 11 Term 2		Chron. Age: 16.1	Candidate Number:

Section A, History of Need		Section C, Profile of LDs	
History of difficulties	Spelling weak		Reading Skills
Level on CoP	Level 2 (SA) in yrs 7 & 8		**1. Reading Accuracy**

Section A, History of Need				Section C, Profile of LDs	
History of difficulties	Spelling weak			Reading Skills	
Level on CoP	Level 2 (SA) in yrs 7 & 8			**1. Reading Accuracy**	
KS 3 NCT scores:	E	M	Sc	**Name of test**	WRAT4
				Test ceiling	95 years
Previous Assessment? Dyslexic, Yr 7	**By whom?** Independent EP			**Date of admin**	Year 11 Term 2
				S.Score	104
Screening Tests				**Reading age**	17.8
Name of test	**Score**			**Comments**	Sounds and blends unknown words
				2. Reading Speed & Comprehension	
				Name of test	Edinburgh 4
				Test ceiling	16.6
Learning Support?	Some spelling support in Yr 8			**Date of admin**	Year 11 Term 2
				Speed wpm	
Previous Access Arrangements? **(Date & Exam)**	No			**Speed S.S.?**	
				Compreh S.S.	Set time 103 RA 16.7 / ET 104 RA 17
				Comments	Small increase with ex time
Normal way of working:	In ability group 2, no support			**Writing Skills**	
National Curriculum Levels				**3. Spelling assessment**	
Subject:	**Level:**			**Name of test**	Graded Word Spelling Test
English	7/8			**Test ceiling**	17.5
Maths	7/8			**Date of admin**	Year 11 Term 2
Science	7			**S.Score**	85 SA13
Geog	6			**% unrec words**	None
Bus Studies				**Comments**	Reasonable phonic approxim
Food Tech	7/8			**4. Writing Speed**	
Art				**Free wr, wpm**	16.4 wpm
RS	8			**% unrec words**	None – though 20% incorr
French	7			**Dict/WP wpm**	38 wpm
				Quality of lang	Similar to free writing
				Other relevant info	

Compreh S.S.: Set time 103 RA 16.7 | ET 104 RA 17

Section B, Recommendations	
1	Allow 10% extra time to check through spellng on written papers
2	
3	

Other relevant info

<u>CATs Year 7 Term 1 Verbal Reasoning</u>
<u>Standard score 103 Non VR 115</u>

CTOPP rapid naming tests, Digit: **SS 9 (1-20 scale) Percentile 37,** Letter: **SS 8 %ile 25,** Object: **SS 8 %ile 25,** Colour: **SS 9 %ile 37.**

Student's comments: Mother has contacted the school to ask for extra time, as she is dyslexic. Diane feels she should be allowed 25% extra time as she writes slowly. (Not picked up in screening as scores in normal range & writing legible.)

Fig. 10.5.2   **Diane's Student Record Sheet, Access Arrangements GCSE etc.**

11. Test Information

Graded Word & Timed Reading Comprehension Tests Compared

(for further information see Chapter 8 & Test References below)

Name of Test / sample size / where & when developed	Age-range; individual or group admin. Scores generated for ....
Access Reading Test / 4000 / UK ; 2006	7 – 20+ years; individual or group Silent reading comprehension
DRA Diagnostic Reading Analysis / 2,800 in toto, incl. 1100 Weak Readers / UK; 2004	7 – 16 years; individual Oral reading accuracy, fluency/reading rate; comprehension
ERT4 Edinburgh Reading Test Fourth Edition / 4,600/ UK; 2002	11.7 – 16.6 years; individual or group Silent reading comprehension**
Edinburgh Reading Test 4 – Interactive	11.7 Years – Adult; individual (On-Screen) As ERT4**
HGRT Hodder Group Reading Tests – Second Edition / 5982 / UK ; 2007	5 – 16+ years; group Silent reading comprehension**
HORT Hodder Oral Reading Tests / 1300 / UK; 2006	5 – 16 Years 9 Months; individual Oral word reading; sentence reading; speed of reading
SWRT (6-16) Single Word Reading Test /1300/ UK; 2006	6 – 16 years: individual: Oral word reading
WIAT II-UK-T Wechsler Individual Achievement Test / 892 / UK; 2006	6 – 16 years 11 months (USA norms up to 85 years are included); individual Oral word reading; reading comprehension; reading speed; spelling
WRAT 4 Wide Range Achievement Test 4 / 3000 / USA; 2006	5 – 94 years; individual Oral word reading; spelling; arithmetic
WRAT-E Wide Range Achievement Test – Expanded Individual Assessment Form I / 8000 / USA; 2001	7 – 24 years 11 months; individual (Level 5 covers 14 – 18 years 11 months) Oral reading comprehension; listening comprehension; oral expression; written language, maths
WRAT-E Wide Range Achievement Test – Expanded Group Assessment Form G / 8000 / USA; 2001	7 – 18 years 11 months; group (Level 5 covers 14 – 18 years 11 months) Silent reading comprehension; maths; nonverbal reasoning**

** A time limit is set for these tests, so fluency is a factor in overall performance, but a reading speed score is not generated.

Test References

Access Reading Test, 2006, McCarty, C. and Crumpler, M. Hodder Murray

Adult Reading Test (ART), 2004, Brooks, P., Everatt, J. and Fidler, R., Harcourt Assessment

Assessment of Handwriting Speed, 2001, Allcock, P., Patoss website www.patoss-dyslexia.org

Beery Buktenica Visual Motor Integration Test (VMI) 5th Edition, 2004, Beery, K.E., Buktenica, N. A., & Beery N.A., Ann Arbor Publishers

British Picture Vocabulary Scale – 2nd edition (BPVS), 1997, Dunn L. & Dunn L., NFER Nelson

Comprehensive Test of Phonological Processing (CTOPP), Wagner R., Torgeson J. and Rashotte C., Harcourt Assessment

Detailed Assessment of Handwriting Speed (DASH), 2007; Henderson,S, Barnett,A and Scheib,B. Harcourt Assessment

Diagnostic Reading Analysis, 2004, Crumpler, M. & Mc Carty, C., Hodder Murray

Digit Memory Test, Rev. 2002, Ridsdale J. & Turner M., Dyslexia Action [http://www.dyslexiaaction.org.uk/Administration/uploads/digit.pdf] *t*

Dyslexia Screening Test – Secondary (DST-S), 2004 **& Dyslexia Adult Screening Test (DAST),** 1998, Fawcett A. & Nicholson R., Harcourt Assessment

Edinburgh Reading Test 4, 2002, Educational Assessment Unit, University of Edinburgh, Hodder Murray

Gray Oral Reading Tests (GORT-4), 2000, Wiederholt, J. Lee and Bryant B.R., Harcourt Assessment

Gray Silent Reading Test (GSRT), 2002, Wiederholt, J. Lee and Blalock, G., Harcourt Assessment

Helen Arkell Word Spelling Test Part 1 (HAST),1998, Brooks, P.L. and McLean, B., Helen Arkell Dyslexia Centre

Hodder Group Reading Tests, Second Edition, 2007, Vincent, D. And Crumpler, M. Hodder Murray

Hodder Oral Reading Tests, 2006, Vincent,D. and Crumpler,M. Hodder Murray

Morrisby Manual Dexterity Test, part of Morrisby Profile 1991(revised), Morrisby, J.R., Morrisby, M.J., Fox, G.D.,The Morrisby Organisation

Movement Assessment Battery for Children (Movement ABC) 2nd Edition, 2007, Henderson, S.E. & Sugden, D.A., Harcourt Assessment

Naglieri Nonverbal Ability Test, 2002, Naglieri, J.A., Harcourt Assessment

Nonword Reading Test, 2004, Crumpler, M. & McCarty, C., Hodder Murray

Peabody Picture Vocabulary Test III, 1997, Dunn, L., and Dunn, L., nferNelson

Perins Spoonerism Test, 1983, Perin D, Available from Dyslexia Action website [http://www.dyslexiaaction.org.uk/Administration/uploads/perins.pdf]

Phonological Assessment Battery (PhAB), 1997, Fredrickson, N., Frith, U. & Reason, R., nferNelson

Ravens Progressive Matrices & Vocabulary Scales, 2008, Raven, J.C., Court, J.H., Raven, J, Harcourt Assessment

Sentence Completion Test, Hedderly, R., Available from Dyslexia Action website [http://www.dyslexiaaction.org.uk/Administration/uploads/sentence.pdf]

Single Word Reading Test, 2007, Foster, H. nferNelson

Symbol Digit Modalities Test (SDMT), 1982, Smith, A., Available from Dyslexia Action website [http://www.dyslexiaaction.org.uk/Administration/uploads/digit.pdf]

Test of Word Reading Efficiency (TOWRE), 1999, Torgesen, J.K., Wagner, R.K. & Rashotte, C.A., Harcourt Assessment

Vernon Graded Word Spelling Test, 3rd Edition, 2006, Vernon, P.E. , Hodder Murray

Wechsler Individual Achievement Test, Second UK Edition For Teachers (WIAT-II-UK-T), 2006 Harcourt Assessment

Wide Range Achievement Test – 4th Edition (WRAT4) 2006, Wilkinson, G.S., Harcourt Assessment

Wide Range Achievement Test III – Expanded Edition (WRAT-E), 2001, Wilkinson, G.S., Harcourt Assessment

Wide Range Intelligence Test (WRIT), 2000, Glutting, J., Adams, W. and Sheslow, D., Harcourt Assessment

Wordchains, Guron, L..M., 1999, Teachers Guide 2006 nferNelson

Working Memory Test Battery for Children (WMTB-C), 2001, Pickering, S. & Gathercole, S., Harcourt Assessment

Some source contact websites:
- Ann Arbor www.annarbor.co.uk
- Dyslexia Action www.dyslexiaaction.org.uk
- Harcourt Assessment www.harcourt-uk.com
- Helen Arkell Dyslexia Centre www.arkellcentre.org.uk
- Hodder Murray www.hoddereducation.co.uk
- The Morrisby Organisation www.morrisby.co.uk
- nferNelson www.nfer-nelson.co.uk
- Patoss www.patoss-dyslexia.org

12. Frequently Asked Questions

MEANS OF ACCESS TO THE EXAMINATION (i.e. READING)

1. If the candidate does not qualify for a reader, is there anything we can do?

The JCQ booklet includes an arrangement for candidates who are refused readers to sit in a separate room with an invigilator and simply to read the questions out loud. The invigilator makes no comment and the candidate does not have to read loudly enough for the Invigilator to hear but only to be able to listen to his or her own voice. This reduces pressure on the candidate who panics when watching other candidates in a large hall working more quickly. It also helps them to concentrate and to focus on self-correction. Many candidates know that the word they have read is out of context and, if they know the subject matter, will be able to link the sound to the most appropriate word for that sentence. Candidates who regularly practise reading aloud will find this even more helpful and it will encourage independent reading. 'Read aloud' is a Centre delegated arrangement.

2. How can we help a candidate with language disorder who cannot understand the questions?

As comprehension is part of the examination, there is no possibility of having any explanation or guidance given. It is very hard, especially when a degree of autism is involved, as the candidate does not understand why help has been given throughout the teaching time but is not available during the examination. The new regulations allow below average scores in comprehension to be taken into account when permitting a reader or an oral language modifier if that represents the candidate's normal way of working in subjects not testing reading. The candidate does not then have to decode and comprehend at the same time.

3. Can bi-lingual candidates have a reader?

No. Only those who also have reports showing evidence of learning difficulties with a history of need and a history of provision. These will be candidates who also have problems in their own language and/or who have been in the UK long enough to improve their English but are prevented from doing so by other cognitive deficiencies.

4. Which tests of reading speed and comprehension cater for the 16 – 19 age group?

See Chapter 11, *Test Information*.

5. Where can we find age-appropriate materials for adults?

The WRAT (Psychological Corporation) has norms up to 75 years; TOWRE & CTOPP (ProEd) go up to 24 years (For full references, see Chapter 11). Subtests from the DAST (Psychological Corporation) could be useful. I notice in their catalogue a new entry – Gray Silent Reading Tests (of comprehension) with an age range from 7 up to 25 years. Further tests suitable for adults are listed in the DfES SpLD Working Party 2005 report which can be seen from the Patoss website.

MEANS OF PRESENTING RESPONSES (i.e. WRITING)

6. What criteria do you apply in deciding whether to allow a scribe?

Legibility is usually not the only factor. If it were, Centres could provide a transcript of the candidate's script, as long as the usual teaching staff can read the script, of course. A scribe is more appropriate where there is a combination of very poor legibility, incomprehensible spellings or grammar and the inability to express oneself and to put the content of the answer down on paper. A telling indicator might be three or four lines of primary school English produced by the candidate writing independently, compared to a whole page of a typical sixteen year old talking to someone else. The difference in the content is startling. Awarding Bodies no longer require samples of writing to be submitted.

7. Can the scribe use a word processor so that the candidate can see what is being written?

Yes. The scribe must write down, or word process answers exactly as they are dictated. Separate invigilation is required.

8. Is it possible for a candidate who requires a scribe to use a voice recognition machine?

A request to use voice recognition software would be considered in the same way as a request to use a scribe. The Scribe Cover sheet would have to be placed on the script.

9. How can we determine which criteria should be applied when requesting a word processor?

The word processor can be used by a candidate whose disability/learning difficulty impairs handwritten communication or whose handwriting is illegible. It should be the candidate's normal method of working and the candidate should be proficient in its use.

10. Is there a standardised test of writing speed?

Yes! See Chapter 8.

11. What is the normal handwriting speed for candidates taking GCE units?

A definitive answer is not possible at present. However, see Chapter 8 for a discussion and the Patoss website for projected figures.

POLICY & SYSTEMS WITHIN CENTRES

12. Inclusion policies lead to requests being made for arrangements which are not appropriate for the assessment, on the grounds that funding has been sought to include the candidate, therefore they must take the examination.

Decisions must be made and advice given at the start of the two year course, about what the candidate who has been included on a course, can realistically expect to achieve. If it is made clear from the start that there is a difference between inclusion on a course and the possibility of assessing skills which have to be performed independently, then much heart-ache is spared. Examinations always differentiate between those who can and those who cannot demonstrate the knowledge, understanding and skills which are being assessed. This applies equally to all candidates who take examinations. Under the DDA, there is no duty to make a reasonable adjustment in respect of the application of competence standards.

13. What is the difference between an access arrangement and a reasonable adjustment?

The vast majority of candidates who need access arrangements are not disabled under the terms of the Disability Discrimination Act and probably have learning difficulties or very mild forms of disability. The Act relates to substantial impairment only. JCQ Awarding Bodies have included candidates with moderate learning difficulties for many years. Access arrangements are a defined list of assistance which may be given according to need and according to the assessment objectives being tested. There must be clear evidence of need in the report submitted with the application. Candidates with substantial disability who can establish that they are protected by the Act will be permitted reasonable adjustments, many of which will be the same as the access arrangements listed in the JCQ regulations but some of which may be personal to the individual candidate. Their adjustments will be considered in the context of the competence standards being tested in the knowledge, understanding and skills required in the assessment objectives and in the context of reasonable costs and reasonable resources. The security and integrity of the examination must be maintained and it would not be considered reasonable to make an adjustment which invalidated the candidate's results.

14. Are cognitive tests necessary for adults?

They might be helpful if the adult has no formal qualifications and left school a long time ago, but they are not required.

15. Should access arrangements be given to those who do not attend school?

The candidate is eligible for access arrangements if the learning difficulty has a substantial effect on performance. This may be the case when a candidate does not benefit from full time education, but it is not the reason which matters as much as the effect. If the candidate does not attend the course, it is the level of attainment which is lowered and there are no access arrangements which can make up for lack of knowledge and skills.

16. Is some interpretation allowed in transcripts?

The transcript must be word for word an exact copy of the candidate's script. The purpose is to produce a legible version of what the candidate has written. Where a candidate has spelt a non-technical word incorrectly, the transcriber may correct it in the transcript but must not insert or omit any words, nor alter their order. Technical terms must not be corrected.

17. Do we need psychological assessments to be done when only 25% extra time is allowed by the Centre?

YES! Many Centres have misunderstood these regulations because they have not read the page in the Joint Council booklet on Access Arrangements which relates to the delegation of extra time to Centres. When the Centre gives the extra time, evidence must be in their files to show that the candidate has either a Statement based on psychological assessment by the Local Authority or one provided by an Educational Psychologist or appropriately qualified teacher. The report, for these purposes, does not have to be written within the two-year period but during the secondary school period. When medical emergencies arise, medical information should be kept on file. Extra time is not appropriate for every illness, only for those injuries or conditions which slow down the candidate during the examination.

18. How should we deal with parents who demand extra time when it is not needed?

The Joint Council booklet makes it clear that the time allowance should be related to need and that up to 25% should be given. It also points out that candidates might need extra time in one paper and not in another. Not all candidates have to be given the full amount. It should be related to their degree of need. It is a good idea to measure how much time the candidate spent on each mock examination and to explain to the parents that keeping a candidate in the examination room when the paper is finished is not helping anyone. All arrangements agreed must reflect the candidate's normal way of working.

19. Some dyslexics are very bright and have scores way above the norm but with a considerable discrepancy between performance and verbal ability or between what they would have been expected to achieve and their attainment.

For most of these, up to 25% extra time will suffice. It should be remembered that an arrangement or adjustment must be effective or there is no point in making it.

20. How do Colleges obtain evidence of a history of need?

The JCQ report form is meant to act as a passport to access arrangements which travels with the candidate from one Centre to another. When the candidate applies for admission, you can request a copy of the form which will contain the history of need and the history of provision.

21. How much time should be allocated to writing reports?

If the form is filled in at the beginning of the course, it can be updated section by section until the application is submitted. You need to fill in enough sections to establish the nature of the problem.

22. Some Awarding Bodies have insisted on new applications for arrangements at AS.

One application will last for the whole of a two year course, as long as the application contains all the subjects being entered, all the arrangements required and the report is valid for the two years. If the candidate was assessed more than two years before the examinations or changes Centre, or courses, or levels of qualification, a new application will be necessary.

23. Sometimes we cannot meet the deadlines for submitting applications because a candidate joins the course late.

It is always a problem to encourage people to meet the deadlines without being too inflexible when they cannot. The difficulty is that sometimes "late" means "too late". It is a good idea to prioritise your cases. Is this candidate taking an early assessment which could be taken at another time? Is there a terminal assessment which cannot be put off? If a modified paper is required, the Boards will not be able to produce one very late, however willing they are to help. If you keep on top of applications for your regular candidates, it is not so daunting when there are one or two late ones. What the Awarding Bodies cannot manage is thousands of late applications which all come in just between Easter and the day of the examination, by which time we are on the phones all day and cannot process the paperwork.

24. How can we cut down on paperwork?

Modernisation should achieve this in the not too distant future. Two phases of the NAA computer site are already up and running. In the meantime, try to have candidates assessed at the beginning of the two year course and make one application for the whole course.

13. Access Arrangements for Key Stage 2/3 National Curriculum Tests

By Caroline Read

Teachers often ask why there are procedural differences regarding access arrangements during Key Stage assessments and public examinations. This article briefly addresses that issue.

Access arrangements for National Curriculum Tests (more commonly, but incorrectly known as 'SATs'), are the same as those available for GCSE etc. However, the criteria for allowing each arrangement, and the methods for application are quite different.

State schools must apply to their Local Authority assessment co-ordinator, and public schools to the National Assessment Agency (a subsidiary of the Qualifications and Curriculum Authority) for permission for students without a statement of SEN to have up to 25% additional time, for statemented and non-statemented students to have *more than* 25% additional time, and for papers to be opened more than one hour before the start of the test, for whatever reason. No specialist qualification is required to complete the application which must be made on-line.

Pupils are required to meet a certain number of criteria before a school will be given permission to allow additional time.

Arrangements which can be allowed at the discretion of the school include: readers, amanuenses, signers and communicators, prompters, transcripts, use of a word processor and rest breaks. Like the JCQ regulations there is a stress on normal classroom practice, arrangements should not be put in place just for the tests.

The reason that the two sets of regulations are at variance is simply that they have developed quite separately. The NC tests and the JCQ general qualifications have different purposes, and are administered by different organisations.

The NC tests are designed to demonstrate how successful a school has been in imparting the National Curriculum to their pupils, and how the school is achieving in relation to a local and a national average. They are not primarily intended to be a test of individual skills. A pupil would not offer his NC test scores when applying for a job, for example.

However, GCSE, GCE, and GNVQ are used to test the skills, knowledge, understanding and competence of an individual candidate in relation to a specific set of assessment objectives, and will be used by the individual to demonstrate that he is capable of carrying out a job of work or taking part in further education. For this reason the method for applying for most arrangements is far more rigorous.

> Reference:
>
> **Assessment and Reporting Arrangements KS2/3 2008**
>
> Qualifications and Curriculum Authority

Dyslexia? Assessing and Reporting, The Patoss Guide

Edited by Gill Backhouse and Kath Morris

This book focuses on the purposes, principles and practicalities of assessing for dyslexia across successive age groups, exploring the changing assessment issues and specific assessment needs.

Assessments are needed to diagnose, to plan intervention, to inform school/college policies, to support claims for funding, to justify special access arrangements in examinations, and more. These very different purposes require Specialist Teachers and support managers to have a firm grasp of relevant legislation and professional guidelines, to select appropriate assessments and provide reports that will meet their intended purpose.

Dyslexia? Assessing and Reporting will enable you to achieve this! Down to earth, and with numerous examples, this book provides the practical guidance needed by Specialist Teachers and educational professionals in training, as well as by SENCOs and learning support staff working in schools and colleges.

It looks at the available types of assessments at each stage, explaining how to interpret results and how and when to involve other professionals. Throughout, special emphasis is placed upon the need to cooperate and communicate effectively with others—pupils/students, their parents, class teachers, administrators and fellow professionals—to ensure that appropriate intervention and follow-up support are forthcoming.

Edited by Gill Backhouse and Kath Morris who have both been involved as external verifiers for the OCR SpLD Training Programmes, this book also features contributions from a wealth of other specialists to cover all age ranges. It aims to share good practice throughout the assessment process.

Published by Hodder Murray in association with Patoss,
.

Available from Bookpoint Ltd, Hodder Murray Direct Services,
FREEPOST OF 1488, Abingdon, Oxon, OX14 4YY
Tel: 01235 827720   Fax: 01235 400454   Email: schools@bookpoint.co.uk
Paperback, 208 pp,   Price £17.50   ISBN 978 0 340 90019 2

How Dyslexics Learn
Grasping the Nettle

by

Dr Kate Saunders and Annie White

Recognising learning strengths is a key element to successful teaching. This book concentrates on the successful strategies dyslexics have used and the positive traits associated with dyslexic learners.

"By dyslexics for dyslexics of all ages, this is the first book on the subject which one can honestly say is without fault. This book is full of practical and imaginative examples of 'How to…'. Above all, it shows the learning process for what is truly is – fun!

Susan Parkinson
Arts Dyslexia Trust

"This book is cool…. I don't usually like reading, but I found this book really interesting. I just wish it had been around when I was at school and that my class teacher had read a copy. Then I might not have had to stay in every playtime to practise my handwriting and work on my spelling."
Jonathan Pitts
Artist

"It's readable, practical, realistic, inspirational and humbling. I will definitely be putting the ideas to use and recommending it to friends and colleagues far and wide. My only regret is I didn't read it earlier!'

Susan Cunningham
Class Teacher, Scotland

"With topics ranging from letter formation and tricky times tables to preparing for national exams, this book covers a lot without overloading its readers. It's the sort of book you need to put your name on right away because your colleagues will keep wanting to borrow it!
Maggie Powell
Hospital Teacher for Special Magazine

Chapters include:

Place in a Sunny Position – Convey the potential of the dyslexic learner

Dig a Little Deeper – Discover how dyslexics learn most effectively

Be Creative with Colour – Use imagination when teaching spelling

Cut Out the Dead Wood – Reading for a purpose

Plant Out in Neat Rows – How dyslexics learn handwriting

Deal with Garden Pests – Teach dyslexics to prepare for examinations

Gardening by Numbers – How dyslexics learn mathematics

Forcing Rhubarb – Working within the National Literacy Framework

Written to be easily understood by teachers of dyslexic learners, other professionals working in the field, non-specialist teachers, parents and adult dyslexics it avoids technical jargon. The excellent colour illustrations help bring to life the multimemory techniques described in this refreshing resource.

Available from Patoss, www.patoss-dyslexia.org
Tel: 01386 712650   Fax: 01386 712716   email: patoss@evesham.ac.uk
101pp, paperback   ISBN 0 9539315 1 X
Price £19.95 plus £2.75 packing and postage